Beyond the Rat Race

Beyond the Rat Race

Arthur G. Gish

HERALD PRESS
Scottdale, Pennsylvania
Kitchener, Ontario

TO
DANIEL PAUL GISH

SIMPLE GIFTS

It's a gift to be simple,
It's a gift to be free,
It's a gift to come down where we ought to be,
And when we see ourselves in a way that's right,
We will live in a valley of love and delight!

When true simplicity is gained,
To live and love we will not be ashamed,
To laugh and to sing will be our delight,
Till by laughing and singing
We come 'round right.

From an old Shaker hymn

Dearly beloved friends, these things we do not lay upon
you as a rule or form to walk by; but that all, with the
measure of Light which is pure and holy, may be
guided; and so in the Light walking and abiding, these
things may be fulfilled in the Spirit, not from the letter,
for the letter killeth, but the Spirit giveth life.

Postscript on a Quaker discipline
written by the elders at Balby, 1652

Table of Contents

Leisure
Work
Smoking, Drinking, and Drugs

Preface

SOMEONE ONCE ASKED A QUAKER ABOUT HIS group's beliefs and their work for peace. After hearing what the Quakers were doing, he inquired, "Why don't you preach what you practice?" Many groups and individuals have been quietly living the simple life but have not said much about it. This book is an attempt to proclaim what many people have been practicing.

Simplicity is not a lost dream, but a recurrent vision by which people live. Many religious groups in the past have made it an important part of their teaching. Today many young people raised in affluence are rejecting the dominant materialistic values of our society. As we begin to experiment with a new style of life, it is important to think through the foundations of our values and commitments.

This book examines the need for simplicity, presents a theological and philosophical basis for it, and suggests ways the simple life can become an exciting venture for you. This is a sequel to my first book, *The New Left and Christian Radicalism*, and assumes much that I argue more carefully there. Here I am applying the radical theology of revolution to the area of life-style, showing both the personal and political implications of a life lived in complete faithfulness to Jesus Christ.

I am indebted to many people for all the help I received in writing this. There are those whose simple lives have deeply touched my own. There is my wife, Peggy, with whom life has been an exciting venture and who has given much help and direction to this book.

My thanks also to Dora and Tom Armstrong, Christoph Arnold, Peter Blood, Tim Bowman, Ginny Coover, Dale Brown, John Pairman Brown, Ken Brown, Peggy and Walter Crosby, William Eerdmans, Vernard Eller, Bill Faw, Chalmer Faw, Lois Gish, Charlotte and Bill Kuenning, Kerby Lauderdale, Sharon Long, Elsie and Wesley Mast, Leon Neher, Marge and Ed Polling, Paul Schrock, Art Weiser, Nancy and Paul Williams, Terri and Jeff Wright and Ellrose Zook for their critical comments.

I feel keenly the need to live a life somewhat consistent with what I say to others and so, to share in the menial labor and not oppress someone else, I typed the manuscript myself. In an attempt to deal with my own male chauvinism, I was careful not to use male pronouns unless they specifically referred to males.

Hopefully this book will help you bring your own life-style into closer harmony with your ideals. It will continue to be a real challenge for me.

Art Gish

Introduction

I AM OFTEN ASKED AS I TRAVEL WITH MY husband, "Don't you worry about not having enough money? Isn't it hard to live without knowing how much income you will receive in the coming months?"

The real questions underlying these surface ones are "Do you agree with your husband on this simple life kick, or is it something he forces on you?" and "Can you, as a wife who faces the day-to-day practicalities of running a household, joyfully live a simple life?"

To all this I can honestly answer that I do not see it as being any sort of hardship. I am confident that more money or possessions would not make me feel any more secure.

I am not suggesting that we have achieved a completely simple life-style and no longer have any worries or conflicts. Many others have gone much farther along this path than we have. The simple life, however, should not be kept somewhere at a distance and considered only as an impractical ideal. I believe it can be a rewarding and adequate way of approaching the practical everyday problems of living.

Money and possessions do not deserve such a high priority in our lives that all else is centered around acquiring and maintaining them. The more we are able to free our lives of unnecessary clutter, the richer our lives can become.

Art and I first became involved with simple living while we were in college with little money. There we learned to live on a meager budget, buying only bare essentials. We did not consider this a hardship, for we learned more simple pleasures and grew closer together. It would have been easy for us to raise our standard of living after completing college, but we decided then to continue the same style of life. We felt there was too much value in simple living to give it up.

The simple life is difficult to define clearly. If we recommend specific actions, it is easy for others to see these suggestions as legalistic rules, burdensome if imposed on someone else. But to describe simple living as an attitude and an approach to life without giving concrete and specific examples seems too general and idealistic.

Art struggled with this dilemma as he tried to write about the simple life. He included many suggestions and personal examples to make the message clearer at the risk of being considered legalistic, egotistical, dogmatic, or proud.

When we accept the premise that we could be happier and freer by living a more simple, uncluttered life and begin to experiment with new patterns, we soon realize that this path towards freedom is a continual struggle, a pilgrimage. It is not something we can achieve once and for all by following certain steps and rules. Each of us has our own weaknesses and strengths and individual tastes and needs and will move ahead in different areas of our lives.

To change our life-style completely on our own may be quite difficult. This is why the resources of Christian faith and commitment and finding a community of support are so important. In fact, simplicity is an outgrowth of these relationships.

Important, too, are the implications of simple living to the larger society. Here it is necessary to analyze our growing allegiance to technology, our whole consumer economy, and the underlying assumptions and patterns of capitalism. We must reconsider the increasing control we have allowed these forces to take over our lives and society.

The simple life could not be dealt with adequately without examining the message of the ecological movement and the plea of the poor and oppressed of the world for justice. Somehow the hope that people will move toward simplicity as they find themselves ready to realize these changes in their lives needs to be balanced with the imperative of simplicity for the very survival of humanity.

My husband and I believe that simplicity can be a way of living out our responsibility to our brothers and sisters around the world and at the same time a joyful expression of a more liberated Christian life.

PEGGY FAW GISH

The Poverty of Affluence

A SALESMAN ONCE VISITED A HERMIT WHO WAS living leisurely in the mountains. Informed by the recluse that he would make no sales there, the salesman tried to point out to the hermit the folly of his ways. "Just think," he argued, "If you worked hard like I do, you could earn and save lots of money. When you are older, you could retire and live leisurely without needing to work."

"What do you think I'm doing now?" the man replied.

Everyone wants to live the good life. We strive, search, plot, sacrifice, and even kill to grasp it and enter some vanishing paradise. But somehow it seems always to escape us. We are as unsure how to find that good life as we are confused about what it is. Not only do we not know how to get there, we do not even know the address.

Affluent western society has given us one clear path to the promised land. The formula sounds simple. Work hard, earn lots of money, and consume as much as possible. Be successful, achieve status, get to the top. Why is it, however, that in the most affluent society on earth there is so much boredom and emptiness? Why in the midst of plenty should there be such a famine of meaning, identity, and relationships? Why are people so hungry for something deeper that they will pay fifty dollars for a weekend encounter group?

Affluence has not meant the liberation of human creativity and self-realization, but a new form of slavery and dehumanization. People demand continual novelty, yet tolerate incessant dullness. There are

19

plenty of gadgets, but little meaning and purpose. Because our goals are quantitative, our lives have little quality.

Increasingly we accept shallow materialistic standards as the definition of the good life, gearing our lives for consumption rather than creative living. Because we equate standard of living with scale of consumption, we work harder and harder to produce more and more to become increasingly comfortable, yet find no comfort. We have too much of everything except our virtues. We live in the poverty of affluence.

In our striving we act much like a beast of burden which responds obediently to each new call to duty. We consider our empty lives normal. The pressures society puts upon us we call "reality" and adjusting to them we consider "maturity." The rat race seems to be self-justifying, its goodness self-evident.

We allow our consciousness to be molded to contemporary form without even being aware of it. It also seems as if our society were designed to break the human spirit. Rather than a style of life, it might be called a style of death.

Look at our society. What is its meaning and purpose? A deep affirmation of life and human decency is something we have difficulty accepting. Materialism is at the heart of our values. Instead of the Franciscan or Buddhist ideal of a rich boy who voluntarily becomes poor, the modern hero starts out poor and becomes rich. That is success. Our god is money and Horatio Alger his christ.

Is this the good society? A society in which the majority of people are overwhelmed by the steady stream of consumer goods and end up not only enslaved by them, but also anesthetized against moral choice, spiritual depth, and creative relationships?

Because we have limited reality to the sensory and material, we have left unexplored whole areas of experience and reality. We have a highly developed technology, but a low level of freedom, interrelatedness, and community. We are underdeveloped in our ability to love, care, and share.

Our society is becoming increasingly ugly. It is a beach strewn with beer cans, a river so polluted it catches fire. Notice the appearance, smell, and noise of our cities. Because of materialism and worship of profit, increasingly the countryside is also being marred. Our people have been vulgarized by continual appeals to indulge in luxuries and trivialities as the capitalist cornucopia pours out its steady stream of polluting trash.

Actually we do not qualify for being a materialistic society, for we do not really enjoy the material world. We have been alienated even from that. We buy things we do not want to impress people we do not like. We use inferior products made by people who do not enjoy making them, sold to us by people uninterested in them, and seldom appreciate them ourselves. We buy junk in cute packages and deal with symbols of pleasure rather than the real thing. As Alan Watts put it, "Just when our mouth was watering for the ultimate goodie, it turns out to be a mixture of plaster-of-paris, papier-mâché, and plastic glue. Comes in any flavor."[1]

In view of the failure of our society to provide either outer or inner peace, we are forced to ask whether there might be other values and styles of life that might be more desirable. An alternative must be found. There must be a better way.

---

[1] Alan Watts, *The Book*, (New York: Pantheon Books, 1966), p. 76.

CHAPTER 1

How to Spend Less and Enjoy it More

IF YOU SEE SOME VALUE IN WORKING TOWARD a simpler life-style, you are probably wondering how it would ever be possible. Modern mass production and the consumer revolution have inspired widespread doubt concerning the validity of this style of life. Many think of it only as a foible of saints and eccentric geniuses. For most people it is not a live option. But it can be done.

Exciting possibilities lie in dropping out of the consumer rat race and experimenting with new styles of living. The good life consists not of getting a larger piece of that rotten consumer pie, but in baking a new pie. Don't just talk about the way life should be. Begin to live that life now and demonstrate what can be done.

Two seemingly contradictory points need to be made. Simplicity does not come easily. To withstand the pressures of society requires constant effort and discipline. On the other hand, relax. You can't force simplicity. Don't try to be something you are not. Simplicity is a gift.

Also be prepared for disappointments, especially from friends. Some will consider you a kook and dismiss you. Others will feel sorry for you. Still others will be thankful you are making this protest so that they do not need to get involved.

Before we go into practical suggestions it must be said that *we are not discussing rigid and unswerving observance of any principles or rules. We are not setting up any absolute standard to be followed, but rather giving suggestions which point to freedom and the good life.* We will not all live on the same plane. How much we consume will depend somewhat on age, occupation, health, climate, and location of residence. We do not all have the same tastes.

To say that something is relative does not mean, however, that there are no standards. In discussing relativity one must always ask, relative to what? With the large percentage of poor in the world there is not much question of where we need to begin to draw the line. Rather than set up rigid rules, standards will be discovered by people as they struggle to live on a responsible level.

Neither is this chapter intended as a list of do's and don't's, but as practical examples of what can be done. Although we begin our discussion with concrete suggestions rather than theory, these are not in and of themselves the essence of simplicity. As we continue our discussion in later chapters we will build the basis for a simple style of life.

It should be reemphasized that one could follow all these suggestions and yet not have simplicity. Simplicity is the result of a new reality in our lives that liberates us from all slavery. Rigidly following a set of austere rules has little to do with simplicity. Nor is simplicity a matter of becoming so economy minded that this becomes the focus of living. Neither is it living frugally to become rich. The outward form will not produce an inner reality, but it can be a joyful expression of it. In later chapters we will think in more depth about this new reality of which these suggestions are merely expressions.

Voluntary poverty is not practiced for its own sake. Otherwise it leads to self-righteousness. It can become a powerful witness, however, if combined with a life of service to others. It can give courage and hope to others to break out of their slavery and it can give power and authenticity to our own lives. In a new way we can recapture the best vision of the Roman Catholic orders. If we are free of financial worries we can use our lives for meaningful purposes. We save time by not wasting it on trivia. By reducing our needs we can get a long term loan from ourselves at no interest to be used to do what we consider important.

No one will accept all the suggestions listed here. *I do not live by all of them myself.* In fact, some of them are contradictory. Some are even trite. But they do point a direction and hopefully some will be helpful to you.[1]

Develop Simple Tastes

It is said that the longest journey begins with one step. So it is with simplicity. There is no one place to begin, but as good a place as any is to simplify our desires. Both our emotional needs for things and our actual physical needs can be simplified. Learn to know the difference between real emotional needs (*e.g.*, cheerful surroundings) and addictions. The complexity of our lives is directly related to our material desires. Most of our real needs are of the spirit, such as meaning, purpose, and friendship. By simplifying our material desires our lives will become less burdensome, Gandhi said,

> Civilization, in the real sense of the term, consists not in the multiplication, but in the deliberate and voluntary reduction of wants. This alone promotes real happiness and contentment, and increases the capacity for service.[2]

Cultivate new values and attitudes. Search for more meaningful goals to take the place of inferior ones. Read literature that points in this direction. Associate

---

[1] For the best practical description of a simple life-style and many helpful suggestions, see Helen and Scott Nearing, *Living the Good Life* (Harborside, Maine: Social Science Institute, 1954).

[2] M. K. Gandhi, *Non-Violent Resistance* (New York: Shocken Books, 1951), p. 46.

with people who have ideals you want to work toward, with people who have pioneered on the way. Get caught up in a cause beyond your own selfish interests. Begin to shut off the consumer propaganda on the media. Discriminate between the important and unimportant. Nurture greater sensitiveness to natural beauty. Begin to act on your values.

Throw away your status hangups. Forget about being respectable in society's eyes. Much of your money now is probably spent to give you respectability. Don't be embarrassed to do things that will save money.

Begin to drop out of the rat race. Think of those things you despise most in the establishment and begin to remove yourself from them. Don't support them or contribute to them any longer. A significant movement has developed in relation to non-cooperation with the war machine. Now we also need to withdraw our support of the consumer system. Think, for example, of how much money is fed into the system just through buying soft-drinks which are of questionable value and perhaps even harmful.

It is in relation to consumption that each person can most affect the economic life of society. Here we can have some control (if we are conscious of it) over our own lives and the forces of production. Many aspects of economic life that used to be dictated by circumstance can now be the subject of conscious decision. As purchasers we can determine the shape of our lives and begin to change our economic system.

Stop buying anything that is unnecessary or will not help you live a fuller life. See how much you gain in comfort, health, and happiness. Before you buy anything, ask if you need it and if it will improve your life in any tangible way. After an impulse to buy something, wait a few days at least before buying it.

Give away all that you do not need. De-accumulate. Most readers of this book could give away half of all their possessions and not really sacrifice anything important. It may be easier to make large shifts and changes than small. When one makes small changes all the other things keep pressing in on one. It is easier to eat the whole bag of potato chips than "just one" chip. Do not underestimate the influence our environment has on us. Be careful to deliberately and wisely choose your physical surroundings in such a way that you will be encouraged to live a simple life.

If you are in business you may need a large amount of money to keep the business going, but you do not need more than anyone 'else to support yourself. You can share all that is left over. But this is not enough. This good work cannot justify any exploitation or injustice in your business. If you continue to operate the business (which may be the thing you should do), the direction of that business should be toward a new way of producing and distributing which does not exploit those involved.

Try living on the level you think everyone in the world could live if there were justice. We must decide at what point faith and fear meet. One < can never achieve total security, nor does one want to be totally without anything.

Limit your income. Instead of scheming how to make more money, start scheming to make less. The less you feel obligated to earn the more freedom you can have. Earn as little as possible and spend as little as possible. If you are on a fixed income, at least your desires do not need to climb with your wages. Learn the joy of giving most of your salary away.

Experiment and temporarily adopt a plan for simpler living. Agree for one month to live on welfare standards. You may not continue after the month, but you will never be the same. Fast for a week. It will change your perspective. For some, budgeting is helpful. Make a budget and cut out the fat. Your budget will tell much about your values.

Eat Sensibly

Half the families in the United States, at every level of income, are undernourished. We get more than enough calories, but the wrong kind. Watch what people buy in the supermarket and you will understand why.

An important rule is to not buy "junk food." It is not only a waste of money but also unhealthy. Avoid soft drinks, potato chips, and other non-nutritional items sold as food. These are perfect symbols of the emptiness of consumerism. Eat quality food. My family spends about half as much for food each week as the average family our size, yet we eat much better than most do. We *buy* only good, wholesome food. Generally the most nourishing food is also the cheapest. Many people eat more expensive food, but not as good.

Eating rich foods is not satisfying. One's taste becomes desensitized. When eating simply, each food is appreciated for its own particular flavor. The bland makes the spicy more distinctive. But if everything is saucy, all becomes bland. Fresh water, milk, or fruit juices are far superior to all the artificial tastes that have been huckstered on us by the soft drink people. Taste-ticklers do not satisfy. We keep craving more and more.

Gluttony is also a great problem. Not only is overeating a waste, but it also creates an extra burden for the body. With all the poisons in our food, the more we eat the more poison we take into our bodies. Obesity itself is a large health problem. If we eat less we will enjoy eating more. It is wiser and healthier to eat to live than to live to eat.

Food does not need to be a major item in our budget. We only need a few pounds of food a day. Consider the cost per pound of potatoes, dried beans, corn meal, rice and even vegetables and fruit. And if you buy them in quantities they are only about half the price. If you live in a city take a trip to the country and buy large quantities of food from farmer's markets. Or better yet, go to the farmer and get produce (*e.g.,* fallen fruit) that cannot be sold. Form a co-op and buy things wholesale. Some save money by having a freezer. Prepared foods are expensive, less tasty, and less healthy. I think the tastiest food I eat is the homemade whole wheat bread that I bake. That is real luxury. Eating the plastic stuff sold in stores at high prices is poverty.

Mix powdered milk with fresh milk. You cannot tell much difference. Make a list before you go shopping and stick to it. You will be less tempted to buy luxury items if you do your shopping after eating instead of just before mealtime. Store name brands are usually much cheaper and of equal quality to big name brands. Read labels carefully when shopping. Contents must be listed in decreasing order by weight. If the first item listed is water, reconsider. Don't eat out very often. When going on trips, pack a lunch instead of stopping at restaurants. Eat a good, healthy, and varied diet.

Limit your consumption of meat. No one needs meat twice a day. Meat is a very expensive food. Buy cheaper cuts of meat or become vegetarian. Producing meat is an inefficient way of producing food. It takes many more times the amount of land to produce an equal amount of meat protein as grain. Eat brown rice and whole grains.

Be careful not to eat much food with high concentrations of additives. Hot dogs and lunch meats are especially bad. Learn about health foods.

Cook more one-dish meals. Put it all together in a casserole, stew, or soup. This means less work and less dishwashing. Cook larger amounts and plan for meals of left-overs.

Use parts of food usually thrown away. Many seeds, such as those of squash, are delicious roasted. Vegetable tops and leaves can be cooked. The water in which vegetables have been cooked can be used for soups and stews. And when eating an apple, eat close to the core where most of the vitamins are found. Most people throw away the most nutritious part of the apple and eat the poorer part. The peelings of many vegetables like potatoes contain the most food nutrients.

Grow your own food. Plant a garden. If you live in a city, use cans and flower boxes or find some secluded spot to raise some vegetables. You can grow an indoor garden using artificial light. Try the Chinese practice of growing seed sprouts for food. Be careful not to use poisoned seeds. Soak the seeds overnight. Then keep them moist in a dark place for several days. Rinse twice daily. Soon you will have sweet fresh greens.

Consider the difference in quality of life if everyone had a small garden. Not only would our food be much better, but we would reestablish our roots in the soil and overcome some of our alienation from nature. All of us should have the opportunity to grow some of our own food.

Don't forget all the free food that is available right outside your door, even if you live in a city. Many plants considered weeds are both nutritious and delicious if picked at the right time. Even in the city, you are within a short walk of many tasty greats like dandelion, chick-weed, and wild garlic.[3]

If you eat meat, many wild animals are good, including anything from rabbits, fish, frogs, and crayfish to woodchucks and birds. Even if you live in the city, many animals are available not far away. Be careful to respect conservation laws, however. Walk through parks and forests and gather your own food such as herbs, teas, berries, nuts, roots, and other delicious

[3]For more suggestions, see Oliver Perry Medsger, *Edible Wild Plants* (New York: Macmillan, 1947); Euell Gibbons, *Stalking the Wild Asparagus* (New York: David McKay, 1962); and Sun Bear, *At Home in the Wilderness* (Healdsburg, California: Naturegraph Publishing Co., 1968).

foods. Our friends love our sassafras tea made from roots we dig up in the woods.

A World War II British aviator parachuted to safety in a jungle, but became lost. By the time he was located, he had already died of starvation. Ironically, his body was found in a patch of purslane, a nutritious weed roughly equal in food value to green beans. He had starved to death in the midst of abundance.

Early American settlers sometimes starved rather than eat the diet of the Indians. Liberation involves learning more about nutritious foods and breaking the chains of habit and custom.

Dress Simply

And then there is clothing. Think for a minute about your clothes closets. You do have more than one, don't you? And think about how full they are. You probably need less than half of them and seldom or never wear most of them. Yet you still keep buying more. Almost everyone reading this book has no good reason to buy any clothes for the next two years. You can save a lot there.

Think of all the energy you use shopping for clothes and all the work you do to earn that money. Then think of all the monotonous labor that went into sewing those clothes for you (who said simplicity leads to monotony?). The sewing of clothing in clothing factories is especially dull and boring. We should wear our clothes as long as possible just to make as little as possible of this depressing work necessary. Consider making your own clothes. Make children's clothes from old adult clothes instead of buying new cloth.

If you want to simplify your life, don't follow the fashions. Buy good clothes and wear them until they are worn out. If you need to buy new clothes, buy your winter clothes in the spring and your summer clothes in the fall when they are on sale. Also don't buy many clothes that need drycleaning.

Try Walking

Then there are automobiles. You can likely do without one. If you feel you can't, at least don't buy a new one every year. Keep repairing your old one. That is usually cheaper than buying a new one. Drive as little as possible. Live near your work. Take public transportation whenever it is available.

Walk or ride a bicycle if you are not going far. You will cut down on pollution, save money, and improve your health in addition to avoiding all those traffic jams.

When driving, pick up hitch-hikers. Hitch-hike yourself instead of driving. Think of the inefficiency of the millions of empty seats in the vehicles crowding our highways.

Suppose automobiles were banned from our cities and the streets were made into parks. Wouldn't we gain a higher quality of life?

Always Economize

There are a thousand ways of cutting corners on your living expenses. Here are a few suggestions. You will think of many more.

Whenever possible buy things on sale, but be careful this does not become a rationalization for buying things you don't really need. You might be able to save twenty dollars by buying an item on sale for one hundred dollars, but you could save one hundred dollars by not buying it at all!

Don't throw away anything you can use or that can be given away or sold. Overcome the mania for newness. For those with artistic ability, beautiful art work can be made with junk. Buy old used appliances and furniture. There is a great abundance of old items, perfectly good but somewhat out of style. Many were made before planned obsolescence and are of excellent quality. Friends of ours found a beautiful old gas stove on a trash pile and it works as well as any new one. Often good places to shop are at Salvation Army stores, auctions, or rummage sales. Buy from a previous owner rather than a store. Live in a low-rent area. Move to a less expensive apartment.

Set the thermostat lower in your home and put on more clothes. It will save heating expenses, cause less pollution, and you will be healthier as well. People were never meant to live in hot stuffy rooms. To save both water and heating costs, rinse dishes in a pan of hot water rather than in running water. Turn off lights as you leave a room.

If convenient, instead of buying your own washing machine, consider using a laundermat. It may be cheaper unless you have a large family. Or share a washing machine with neighbors. Don't wash your clothes as often. Maybe you can wear some of them more than once. If possible, hang clothes out to dry. Dryers consume much fuel and energy which means increased pollution.

Don't buy any more insurance than is absolutely necessary. Many people live in forced poverty because of insurance payments.

The cheaper goods are not always the most economical. The more expensive items may be more economical and simple, although this can also be a rationalization. Buy good quality articles that will last a long time, articles that are modestly priced and of reasonably good quality. Then you will not need to buy as much nor as often.

Simplicity does not mean mediocrity, but rather implies quality. If building a new house, build it sturdy, cheaply and simply.

Buy less things but use and enjoy them more.

Enjoy What's Free

Take advantage of as many free things as possible. It is false to say that you cannot get anything for nothing. Most of our basic necessities (life, air, water, sunshine, earth) are free. There is no reason why anyone who is poor cannot live as well as a king. There are free things all around. (We mentioned free food earlier.)

If you enjoy cultural activities, there are many free events all around you. There are free museums, libraries, lectures, movies, concerts, poetry readings, and parks. Check at area colleges for schedules of events. They will have many free recitals, lectures, and films. Volunteer to be an usher at a prestige concert or play. You will get in free. Borrow books, art work, and records from free libraries. They all are available free. Avoid commercial amusements.

Spend more time playing with children. Try smiling at people. Even say hello to them. It's free.

Take a walk in a city on trash day through the affluent neighborhoods and see what you can find. The rich discard most anything. Some people furnish whole apartments that way.

If we are creative, we can almost completely live off the scraps of planned obsolescence. There is a great abundance of technological waste that we can use and easily obtain with little or no money.

This has dangers, however. We are still dependent upon the system. While it is possible to live off the scraps of society if necessary, it is important to see this not as a life-style, but as a means of giving us the freedom to do more important things. Obviously it would not be possible for everyone to live off society's waste. Thus we must use our freedom to begin to develop alternatives to the present means of providing for human needs.

Do It Yourself

Start to make your own things and repair everything you can yourself. Rather than accept innovations, learn to innovate. Part of what it means to be human is to create. Be a creator, not only a consumer. Poverty is to never experience the joy of making and growing things for oneself. Specialization destroys simplicity. We need to recapture our ability to cope with life and handle situations ourselves.

Build your own furniture using simple wooden frames. One can easily make beds, chairs, and sofas by covering them with mattresses and cushions. Build your own house. It doesn't have to be elaborate. Buy things that can be repaired. Instead of buying impersonal cheap greetings cards, make your own. It is fun and will mean much more to those receiving them. Get someone to cut your hair instead of going to barbers and hairdressers.

The question of the amount of time needed for these things is an important one. It is true that one can become a slave to making things for oneself. But it is also important to do some things for ourselves. We waste much time now that could be used creatively.

There are times when simple living will use up some of our physical energy, but our affluence drains our spiritual energy. The main question is whether we are making these decisions for ourselves or letting society make them for us. *We* must decide on priorities.

Some have decided to go the whole way, move to the country, and live close to the earth. Many of them try as much as possible to grow all their own food and make everything they need. We may not decide to go that far, but we can begin making more things for ourselves.

Pool Resources

Much can be saved by borrowing and sharing. In any suburban area, every family has a lawn mower (unless they pay others to cut their lawn) and a thousand other things they do not use most of the time. Why not share more and buy less?

Get together with some friends and share as many items as possible instead of everyone buying their own. This could include anything from vacuum cleaners, to tools, to cars. Share periodical subscriptions. Borrow things from neighbors and friends. But remember always to return them cleaner and in better shape than when you borrowed them. Go the second mile in all sharing arrangements to avoid any arguments or hard feelings that might otherwise arise.

Borrow this book instead of buying it.

Work together with others as much as possible. Practice mutual aid. If you have a straight salary you may even be able to support one or two other families who will give full time to non-salaried work such as peacemaking. Pool salaries and share expenses. This beats insurance.

As the number of people in your community of sharing increases, the number of possible ways of sharing and simplifying your life also increases.

Boycott Gadgets

What about all kinds of modern gadgets, including "time saving" devices? Some machinery is truly time saving, decr ses drudgery, and has a minimum of harmful side effects. We use a washing machine, for example. A "time saving" gadget is fine if it actually saves time and simplifies our lives.

But let's be realistic. Most "time saving" gadgets complicate our lives rather than simplify them and add another monthly payment to our list. Many times we would be better off doing a job manually than using a machine. Often this would save both costs and labor.

Machines are not always as efficient as they seem to be. To avoid machines is to escape the frustration of mechanical breakdowns. One gets good exercise doing a job manually which is an aid to good health. One experiences a greater sense of accomplishment in participating more directly in a project.

Take for example a dishwasher. Considering all that it costs, maybe it would be easier to eat more simply, use only one dish for each person, and serve the food in the cooking utensils. Do we need to use so many dishes each meal that we require a dishwasher which we must work so much extra to pay for and maintain that we have less time to play with our children? It makes one tired even to read that sentence. The simplest thing may be for the whole family to have a good time washing dishes together and spend the rest of the evening playing together. But our gadget-filled lives are too busy for that.

A good rule to follow is never to use a machine when one can as conveniently do the job oneself. Don't drive if you can easily walk. You will feel better and discover many interesting things you have been missing. Don't use elevators unless you are going to the twentieth floor. Boycott some things that are totally unnecessary such as electric can openers and electric knives.

Consider not having a T.V. set. Think of the pollution that is spewed out every minute as people are fed lies and a distorted sense of reality. Not only is it harmful for children and adults, but it keeps both from creative activities. It encourages passivity and creates patterns of dependence on machines for entertainment and stimulation.

Even if all the programming were of excellent quality, television still should be used sparingly. To be liberated from television gives one more time to be with people, more time for reading, more time to participate in meaningful activities. Too often it is used as an excuse for parents not to relate to their children. If one does have a T.V. set, one should be very selective and disciplined in the use of it.

Some have suggested not having a telephone. It is true that the telephone has become an unruly servant, interrupting everything we do, even lovemaking. If we didn't have a telephone, we would have to visit the people we want to talk with. Is it true that life is impossible without it? If so, consider getting rid of it.

Homes should not look like furniture salesrooms, but should provide an atmosphere of warmth, acceptance, and freedom. They should be expressions of who we are rather than of some factory catalog. The best furniture is a piece you made, something that came from a friend or relative, or a serviceable item you found after a long search. You ought to be able to love your furniture in addition to using it.

Boycott everything you do not approve of. To buy something from a business is a vote to keep both that product and business in operation. Your vote counts. As much as possible, boycott harmful products, insensitive corporations, and products unscrupulously advertised. Trading stamps are tricks to get people to consume more. You might refuse to shop at stores that give them.

Travel Light

Vacations also can be simple. There is no reason to head toward the neon lights, costly entertainment, and luxury hotels. You can camp out. All one needs is a sleeping bag and a few bare essentials. Why demand, as many do, all the luxury of home while camping? Learn the joy of simple camping. A relaxing, fulfilling vacation can cost almost nothing. The necessary work can be shared by all involved.

When traveling, stay overnight with friends, relatives, and even friends of your acquaintances whenever possible. Most people appreciate visitors dropping in. Encourage the practice. It is a good way to catch up on news about old friends and to learn more about the area in which you are visiting.

Take a sleeping bag along and don't cause them any more extra work than necessary. Help them with the work. Offer to share financial costs. Invite others to visit you.

Walk the paths least traveled.

Refuse Economic Slavery

Don't give up your freedom. Maintain it. Cherish it. If you really want to remain free, don't go into debt.

Once you have payments to make, the system has you hooked. You don't dare lose your job. You must make those payments. Be very careful with credit cards and charge accounts. They encourage buying more and often carry a high service charge. Consider not having any. Avoid installment buying.

Consider becoming self-employed and working at home. You probably have some skill which you can use to support yourself. Start a cottage industry. Earn only enough to keep going. Use the rest of your time for living and serving others.

Consider living on a part-time job in order to have the flexibility to do what you consider important.

Give up time-consuming rituals such as going to the hairdresser, applying make-up, and washing the car.

Conserve Natural Resources

The simple life means living in an ecologically responsible way. Here are some important ecology suggestions.

Don't waste anything. Natural resources are limited and the production of anything causes pollution. Consume less. Become aware of how your use of anything will affect the environment.

Reuse everything that is reusable. Then reuse it again.

Recycle aluminum, glass, paper—anything that is recyclable. Start a collection center for those items.

Cut down on the use of energy. Power pollutes. Conserve electricity. Avoid using unnecessary electrical gadgets.

Nuclear energy does not appear to be the answer either. The problem of thermal pollution and increased radiation pose great threats. Many claim that the present "permissable radiation emission levels" are unsafe.

Drive less miles and buy smaller engines. Use mass transit or car pools.

Don't buy drinks in disposable containers. Whenever possible buy only returnable bottles and return them. Buy milk in returnable glass bottles. Use containers that disintegrate easily.

Cut down on your use of tin and aluminum cans, especially cans for beverages. Don't buy things in aerosol cans if you can avoid it.

Limit your use of paper and save all waste paper to be recycled. Use both sides of paper. This manuscript was written on used paper with one clean side. Reuse envelopes. Make cloth napkins to reuse and don't use paper towels. Limit your use of paper cups and plates. Avoid the use of any plastics that will soon be thrown away. They do not decompose and burning plastic produces poisonous gases. Don't use plastic cups and tableware. Styrofoam cups are non-degradable.

Don't use pesticides unless absolutely necessary, and then only safe ones. Use organic products rather than commercial fertilizers.

Use only non-polluting soaps.

Save water. Don't take long showers.

Compost leaves and garbage. Don't burn trash.

Boycott all whale products and articles made from other endangered species of animals. Support the preservation of these creatures.

Don't buy jewelry made of precious minerals. Supplies of many of them are being rapidly depleted.

Don't buy a Christmas tree unless it is alive and will be replanted.

Avoid buying a lot of gifts for holidays.

Return junk mail to the sender by writing "refused" on the envelope. It costs the company money and discourages this wasteful practice. Don't support advertizing.

Don't litter.

Don't pollute the air or yourself by smoking.

Be informed on products that are unsafe or pollute. Become involved in political action in the area of ecology and support boycotts of undesirable products. Tell others. Your life and the future of your children depends on it.

***

Yes, it is possible and desirable to simplify our style of living. With little sacrifice the average family can easily save several hundred dollars per year on food. Add to this the savings from driving an older car, not buying as many new clothes, and so on. This can soon add up to a thousand dollars to be used for something worthwhile.

Then add to that all the totally unnecessary expenditures. Meanwhile, the family is healthier and happier. Why not?

Mildred Young challenges us to consider our own lives over against our society.[4]

When society has fed and housed the poor and nursed the sick, and educated the persons of low I.Q. to take a useful place of their own in the economy of man; when the brilliant have been educated for responsibility rather than for personal success; when no persons are standing around rejected and unused while others think themselves entitled to overwork, sometimes priding themselves on being overworked; when war has been renounced and its instruments disassembled . . . when machines are controlled by people and we have outgrown all thought of controlling people by machines—then possibly it will be time enough for Christians . . . to consider whether the world offers any positions of power and success compatible with their convictions.

---

[4]Mildred Binns Young, *What Doth the Lord Require of Thee?*, Pamphlet #145 (Wallingford, Pa.: Pendle Hill Pamphlets, 1966), p. 28.

CHAPTER 2

Simplicity as a Life-style

SIMPLICITY IS A PROCESS NEEDED IN EVERY area of life. We must relate simplicity concretely to all areas of our lives and personalities.

Speech and Thought

A simple life-style includes simplicity of speech and thought. Simple speech implies truthfulness and honesty. Dishonesty complicates. Duplicity is complex. Simplicity avoids deceit. The root meaning of sincere means without wax. It means genuine. That is simplicity.

Simplicity is living with a clear conscience. Consider the entanglement of guilt and all the contortions guilt puts us through. My father says that some people are so crooked that they cannot even lie straight in bed. Simplicity is to live without guilt.

Compare the simplicity of openness to the maze of secrecy. It is the opposite of covering up, justifying, and rationalizing. Because of the duplicity of writing and speaking, glibness of tongue and twisted words, today people have great difficulty knowing the truth about the world we live in. We are faced with the complexity of deception, disguise, and half-truths. It is like a lawyer arguing for his client: "First, my client did not borrow the jug from the plaintiff; second, it was whole when he returned it; and third, it was broken when he borrowed it."

We should say exactly what we mean, no more or less. Tell the truth as you see it. How often we cover up the truth, try to keep from offending people, and say what people want to hear. The result is shallow, inauthentic relationships and lack of trust. Why not be straightforward in speaking the truth? There may be times when we cannot reveal all, but even then honesty can be maintained.

Simply say what you believe. Don't always preface it with a qualification like "It seems to me," "Someone has said, " "I would like to assume that." This is false humility. Actually it is egoistic, for it makes oneself a part of the statement. Just make your statement and let people be free to accept or reject it. If we avoid these qualifications, maybe we will be more careful about the assertions we do make.

Tell it like it is. Don't use euphemisms. Don't say "incursion" when you mean "invasion," "protective reaction" when you mean "hostile attack" or "peace" when you mean "war." Indeed it is frightening to hear our government officials speak and mean the opposite of what they say. There is far too much diplomacy and smooth talking. What a breath of fresh air frankness and candor can be. Follow Jesus' advice and let your yes be yes and your no, no (Matthew 5:37).

Flattery and compliments can be a denial of simplicity. Just tell the person that you accept, love, and care. Forget all the jargon. We might excuse lovers and parents cooing to babies from this, but no one else.

In speech and in writing, state your case as clearly and as simply as possible. Never use a big word if a little one will say it. Big words and long involved arguments are not helpful. The truly educated person can state the most profound truths in such a way that the uneducated can understand them. If you cannot state it simply, maybe you don't really understand it. This is not to recommend imprecise language or sweeping dogmatic statements. Simplicity of speech is not just in finding the shortest or simplest wording, but also in accuracy, openness and, balance. Simplicity implies clarity.

The same applies to thought. Long, abstract, speculative, academic arguments are boring. Besides, they usually indicate an ego trip. Lao-tse said, "Wise men are never scholars, and scholars are never wise men." Much of scholarly activity involves an impractical preoccupation with details and obscurities.

Simplicity does not exclude careful analysis and critical questioning, but it is able to find answers. We all know of intellectuals who have much knowledge, but can never simplify it enough to use it. Overperfection is a denial of simplicity.

Avoid the paralysis of analysis. Some are continually analyzing everything and can never accept anything at face value. Motives are constantly examined. One soon becomes tired of incessant introspection and perpetual philosophizing. It is like the two psychiatrists who met one morning. The one said "Good morning" and the other asked, "What did he mean by that?"

Simplicity is not oversimplification. Oversimplification results in a narrow dogmatic point of view, absolutizing the finite, and ignoring the context. It is the exclusiveness of stressing one point and ignoring other aspects, the attempt to reduce reality to mechanistic processes. Oversimplification is the heresy of most "isms."

Simplicity is the wisdom of moving *beyond* complexity. True simplicity is found on the other side of complexity. Any simpleton can be complicated. It takes wisdom to be simple. Simpletons are simple because they are incapable of dealing with complexity. The wise are simple because in the midst of complexity they can distinguish between the significant and the insignificant. Simplicity is not based on ignorance, but in the deep wisdom of maturity. The process of maturing and growing older is the simplification of life. Simplicity is wisdom. There is no simplicity without wisdom or wisdom without simplicity.

Science and mathematics operate on principles of simplicity. Science gathers a few central principles and conclusions out of a mass of facts. Vast amounts of research are condensed into a few sentences. The more fundamental something is, the more simple it is.

The Swearing of Oaths

Closely related to simple speech is the issue of swearing oaths. Not only in court, but in many other areas oaths are required. Oaths can be involved in anything from getting a driver's license to a required loyalty oath to get a job. Simplicity leads people to refuse to cooperate with this practice.

It is interesting that people are asked to swear on the Bible, a book that flatly forbids the practice. Of course, the church has seldom had trouble dismissing any part of the Bible it finds inconvenient or justifying things clearly condemned by the Bible. Although oaths are not forbidden in the Old Testament, the New Testament is clear in its rejection of swearing.[1]

> Do not swear at all, either by heaven, for it is the throne of God, or by the earth, for it is his footstool, or by Jerusalem, for it is the city of the great King. And do not swear by your head, for you cannot make one hair white or black. Let what you say be simply "Yes" or "No"; anything more than this comes from evil.
>   *Matthew* 5:34-37

Oaths really are unnecessary for the Christian, for telling the truth is not based on such superficial ceremonies. In fact, taking an oath casts suspicion on one's integrity. Does that mean the person will be less honest at other times? If not, why take the oath? Swearing implies a double standard of truth-telling and thus undermines honesty and integrity. To be asked to take an oath is an insult because it infers that a person is a liar but this once should refrain from lying.

---

[1]Additional scripture references are Matthew 23:16-22; Acts 26:25; Hebrews 6:13,30; James 5:12. Also see William Penn, *Treatise on Oaths,* 1675; *Barclay's Apology in Modern English,* ed. Dean Freiday (Phila.: Friends Book Store, 1967), pp. 412-424; Vernard Eller, *The Promise* (Garden City, New York: Doubleday, 1970), pp. 179-188.

Oaths are not only unnecessary, they accomplish nothing. There is no evidence that swearing helps honest people tell the truth or prevents liars from lying. Anyone familiar with a courtroom is well aware of that. The only purpose of the oath is to make a person liable for perjury, but God is not needed for that. God has His own ways of establishing the truth, and they are not the same as those of the state.

Oaths are based on superstition, something Christian faith has done away with. They are based on fear of the wrath of God, a fear that is almost totally absent from our society (not that superstition is absent). Few people are afraid to lie under oath. The theory behind oaths is that God will pay special attention to what we say if we swear. If we lie under oath, God will strike us dead or terribly afflict us in some other way. Supposedly lying when not under oath is not so bad.

Swearing shows a deep lack of respect for God. Every day thousands of oaths are administered in God's name with little concern whether any of the people involved even believe there is a God. The state does not care about God. It just wants something impressive to threaten and scare poor sinners and peasants into telling the truth.

We make a mockery of God by administering the oath even when we know the person will lie. No one is frightened, but we keep going through the motions, using God's name in vain. Sometimes it seems that we even dare God to do something about our rebelliousness against him.

Taking an oath shows a lack of respect for God by attempting to use God's name for our purposes. Rather than seeking to find God's will, we use him to justify our own ideas and goals. God is not a magic formula to be used for our purposes. Jesus understood our blasphemous attempts to make ourselves God and said no to all of them.

For the state to administer oaths is a clear violation

of any understanding of separation of church and state. Why is the state administering religious oaths? Where does it get the authority to do that, either legally or religiously?

It is also appropriate to refuse oaths because we understand our own human limitations. We can never say absolutely that we will do anything, even tell the truth. We never know if we can keep our promise. We do not know the future and it is not in our control. God alone knows the future.

The refusal to take oaths has led many to refuse to relate to secret oath-bound societies (lodges). When one examines their oaths, it is not hard to understand why many Christians refuse to join them.

What we are describing is nothing new. Radical Christians, such as Anabaptists and Quakers, have been refusing oaths for a long time. Those groups which saw the radical implications of the biblical message not only stressed pacifism and simplicity, but also refused to swear oaths. Because of their brave witness, which often involved prison sentences for refusing to swear, it is now legal in the United States to refuse to swear. One can choose to "affirm" rather than "swear." Although there are still some judges who are ignorant of the law and jail people for following the law, you do not need to swear.

We need to begin to ask, however, whether affirming is not avoiding the real issues. To say "I solemnly affirm" instead of "I solemnly swear" is to make a very fine distinction. Jesus said to say yes and no, and nothing more. Most affirming is really a form of swearing. Maybe we should also refuse to affirm.

There is one more area of oaths that we need to examine—loyalty oaths. In spite of how ridiculous oaths are, they are required for employment in many areas, including public schoolteaching in many states. That says something about the school system. And the Supreme Court has declared them to be legitimate, which says something about the Court, also.

In addition to violating Christian teaching, loyalty oaths are utterly worthless and accomplish nothing except keep some people with integrity from teaching. Obviously the only people these oaths would prevent from teaching are people with deep integrity, the very people who should be teaching. A scoundrel would not hesitate to sign them. The only purpose they can serve is to later provide a legal basis (perjury) for firing or jailing, but swearing and oaths are not needed for that.

We also should examine the content of these loyalty oaths. They are stated in various ways, but almost always include the idea of "undivided allegiance" to the government and opposing all enemies of the state.

How could a Christian ever give "undivided allegiance" to the state? That pretty well leaves God out, or at least puts Him second to the state, unless one assumes that the will of the state is always the same as God's will. Many do make this assumption, but not from a biblical perspective. The Bible and history are full of examples of righteous people having to choose between the state and God. In fact, several times, the Hebrew prophets proclaimed God to be the enemy of their nation. Can we oppose *all* enemies of the state? Loyalty oaths, in addition to being ineffective, are an act of rebellion against God.

Silence and Meditation

Simplicity is related not only to speech, but also to the absence of speech. Silence is a necessary ingredient in simplicity. All of us need a period of quiet and silence each day, a time to center- our lives on that which sustains us. We should not always be surrounded by noise and clatter.

Activity and motion can be an intoxicating drug. If the machines stop, we feel an unbearable emptiness. Most of us cannot stand silence or bear to be alone with ourselves. Our lives are driven by a compulsion for noise and activity. Dehumanization creates weak creatures who worship strength and motion. But we need calm and silence. Not an empty silence, but a silence that is rich and full.

The highest power we can imagine is the calm, the sublime. Anyone who has experienced the power of Quaker worship knows the power of silence. Dominic is reported to have visited Francis of Assisi and during their whole visit they never said a word to each other. What a deep encounter that must have been.

Simplicity is to know God. It is the fulfillment that decaying societies and materialism can never satisfy or destroy. The longing for the infinite can be fulfilled only in relation to the infinite. Simplicity is to recognize mystery. People complicate things to deny mystery. Much activity, complexity, and intellectualization is an attempt to escape from God. Simple faith is to live in relation to God rather than speculate about Him.

God is infinitely simple. "Be still, and know that I am God" (Psalm 46:10). It takes a theologian to complicate God. The saints know Him in His simplicity. The simple is found in the beginning, the origin, the source. To be radical is to be simple, for it is to go to the root, to what is basic. To know God is to have everything put in its true perspective. To know God is to know reality.

The ultimate form of simplicity is prayer. In prayer one meets God and sees reality in its true perspective. Clutter falls away, unity is found, and one can respond spontaneously to the source of one's being. The simplicity of prayer is found in openness and responsiveness to the light. "The more a soul simplifies itself, the more God works in it; and conversely, the more God works in it, the simpler does the soul become."[2]

We need a time for silence and prayer. We need to tune our lives to that source of power beyond ourselves. Both our outer and inner lives need to be at-

---

[2]Raoul Plus, *Simplicity* (London: Burns, Oates & Washbourne, 1950), pp. 48, 49.

tentive to the voice of the Spirit. Silence can bring the disjointed pieces of our lives together again. In silence we can find our center and discover new peace, purpose and power.

Titles of Distinction

Simple speech also relates to the use of titles. Is it proper to give some people titles of distinction? On this subject, also, Jesus was clear.

> But you are not to be called rabbi, for you have one teacher, and you are all brethren. And call no man your father on earth, for you have one Father, who is in heaven. Neither be called masters, for you have one master, the Christ.   *Matthew* 23:8-10

The mode of communion in the Church of the Brethren is the "Love Feast" which includes not only the bread and cup, but also feet washing and a communal meal. This is commemorative both of Jesus' last supper and also of the coming great marriage supper of the Lamb, that time in the new age when all will be equal. Somehow it does not seem right for doctors, professors, sirs, and madams to gather around the table. It should only be for brothers and sisters.

Early Quakers refused to use any titles of respect or tip their hats to social superiors. This brought them much trouble. Today radical Quakers and others are refusing to stand in the courtroom when the judge enters. This is not to show disrespect for the judge, but to witness to the belief that no one is worthy of special respect, that all people in the courtroom are worthy of profound respect. To bow before others may be a sign of dishonesty or submissiveness to human authority. People should bow down only before God.

If one accepts the idea of equality, then most titles are illegitimate. Your honor, your holiness, your majesty, your eminence and similar titles are unworthy of any Christian. This applies also to doctor, professor, and reverend. Usually it is the rich, the proud, the ambitious, the hypocrites, or the insecure who desire such titles. Titles are a way of praising and being praised and so encourage vanity (see Matthew 23:6, 7). An attack on pride is really an attack on inequality.

The use of titles is an acceptance of status consciousness and is thus divisive. Most titles imply that the person addressed has authority and power over others. Mister means master. For the most part titles are not used to teach respect, but to teach us to accept the structure of hierarchical relations. They are used to teach us that a person above us is not our brother or sister. The use of titles means perpetuation of inequality and authoritarianism. Either everyone should be given these titles or no one. All of us are under God.

Some argue that in the process of leveling we should level everyone up rather than some down. There is some validity to this, but what is the point of calling everyone doctor? The more titles we add to a person, the further we remove that person from ourselves and from reality. Calling everyone Mr. or Mrs. does not help bring us closer together or teach respect. Respect is not based on the use of titles, but on relationships and concern for all people. Our identity should be found in a reality deeper than a title.

The use of titles also involves dishonesty, for usually the person does not fit or deserve the title. Often people with lofty titles represent the very opposite of their titles. We should not call a dishonorable person "your honor."

Maybe we should also stop using the titles, Mr. and Mrs. They also tend to keep people apart. If any titles are used they should only be brother and sister.

Equality

Simplicity leads a person to consider everyone of equal worth and sees class structure as a sign of the fallen nature of humanity. To live in the kingdom is to reject class distinctions and inequality. The Christian cannot accept old sinful ways. The early Christians abolished all class distinctions among themselves and considered even master and slave to be on the same level. The Christian looks forward to the day when

> Every valley shall be filled,
> and every mountain and hill shall be brought low,
> and the crooked shall be made straight,
> and the rough ways shall be made smooth;
> and all flesh shall see the salvation of God.
> *Luke* 3:5,6.

Christian faith is a leveling process.

We are not discussing an absolute equality that limits creativity and development of potential or denying that there are different roles and gifts. A surgeon needs expensive instruments, a scholar books, a carpenter tools. But do surgeons have any moral right to spend more on themselves than garbage collectors? Having a higher income than our neighbor does not give us any moral right to spend more on ourselves.

Just as most of us have developed a quality of politeness at the family table and do not grab food from others, so we need to see ourselves as part of the human family and begin to care about other's needs.

> I do not mean that others should be eased and you burdened, but that as a matter of equality your abundance at the present time should supply their want, so that their abundance may supply your want, that there may be equality. As it is written, "He who gathered much had nothing left over, and he who gathered little had no lack." *2 Corinthians 8:13-15.*

Equality does not mean that everyone should have an equal opportunity to climb to the top (we do not have that now), but that everyone should be able to participate meaningfully in life. The concept that glorifies the possibility of a newsboy becoming President both ignores social reality and requires equality to be experienced vicariously. If taken seriously as a democratic ideal, it would lead to an inverted pyramid, crowded at the top with successful people, with no support at the bottom because all had abandoned that to rise up the ladder of power. This is unrealistic thinking. It ignores the factors which ensure that only a relatively few will ever come out on top.

Equality has many implications. It means getting rid of hierarchical and bureaucratic relationships in which some people do "significant" and more desirable work and others are forced to do menial tasks. Consider the structure of relationships and work in an office. There is an executive (a man) who considers his time so valuable and important that he hires a secretary (a woman) to do the menial, insignificant tasks that would be a waste of his time. The values here are clear. The executive is far more important than the secretary, and the secretary receives a far lower salary.

Work and relationships do not need to be structured that way. Why can't everyone do both desirable and undesirable work? Everyone should spend some time cleaning toilets and no one should spend a major amount of time doing it. This is not to deny the need for specialization or the fact that we have different abilities, but all should accept some menial physical tasks as a part of their lives.

Scholars, for example, would be better scholars if they had this contact with the real world. Judges should spend some time anonymously in prison before they are given the power to imprison anyone else. If executives and political leaders did some menial tasks and physical labor instead of pushing them on someone down the ladder, maybe they would have less problem with pride and impatience. We do not need to perpetuate hierarchical relationships.

A related despicable practice is the hiring of servants to do our dirty work at a salary much lower than we would ever want to receive for doing more enjoyable work. It is sobering to notice all the black women entering wealthy white suburbs early in the morning. We all know what they will be doing and why.

Everyone should receive an income according to need. Why should some receive (not earn) a million dollars a year and others only two thousand? If there are to be different levels of income, then the highest salaries should go to those doing the least desirable jobs. Obviously, a janitor should receive more than a schoolteacher, and a teacher more than the principal. Don't the teachers consider it more desirable to be teachers than janitors? Of course they do; otherwise they would be janitors.

But we are told that since teachers spent so much time in college getting an education, they deserve more. Is going to college really a sacrifice? For most people college is an enjoyable experience. Maybe those who never had the opportunity to attend college should be given the higher salary to compensate.

All the arguments boil down to the idea that the educated person is worth more than the uneducated one. Who said so? Certainly not God. There is no support for this view in Christianity; nor have I ever heard a moral reason to support it. It is rather a blatant form of racism. It is based on sheer class prejudice, selfishness, pride, and snobbery. How arrogant for some to consider themselves worth more than others!

Jesus told a parable of a man who hired people to work in his vineyard. He hired some in the morning, some at noon, and some late afternoon. But he gave all of them the same pay at the end of the day. Those who did more work protested, but Jesus considered it fair. While this parable concerns the generosity and the grace of God, it is also related to the coming of the kingdom and life within that kingdom. In the kingdom we will be equal, for we will be accepted not on our merits, but by God's generosity.

Simplicity implies giving up our privileged position in the world. To what extent should we accept privileges that are not available to others? We may support all kinds of worthwhile programs and causes, but the real question is whether we are willing to give up our privileged position. That may answer whether we are prepared for radical change in society and the coming of God's kingdom.

Some argue that equality would destroy incentive. The opposite appears to be true. When there is inequality, many people are not allowed to develop their talents and potential. Others are stifled because they are told they are not as important as other people. Oppressed people lose incentive. In the countries where there is the most inequality, people seem to have the least incentive. If incentive and diversity are important, the inequalities which prevent development should be removed.

Others argue that equality would mean monotony. But is there not much variety in any socioeconomic class? In any family where there is freedom for the children, although all have a common and equal background, monotony and uniformity are not the result. People are not like peas in a pod. Equality that involves uniformity is artificial and forced. Equality can never be forced, but is based on freedom.

Sharing

Related to equality is sharing. The extent to which something can be shared determines its worth. The books I value most I want to share with my friends. The most enjoyable activities are those we can share with others, those things we can use without depriving others or taking exclusive possession for ourselves. Consider the thrill of sunsets, mountains, and forests. In intensely personal activities like sexual intercourse we can transcend the acquisitive, impersonal values of our society and find the meaning of sharing. That is why sex is so sacred and not to be misused or turned into a commodity.

To indulge selfishly is to deny the meaning of our existence. We were not created for indulgence, but to love, give, and share. Jesus said, "It is more blessed to give than to receive" (Acts 20:35). It is more enjoyable to share than to accumulate. Acquiring possessions selfishly does not lead to a better life than sharing and cooperation.

This is not to disregard the need for genuine self-love and concern for oneself. We are to love our neighbor *as ourselves*. We should seek the best. But a narrow selfishness will not lead to fulfillment. It is actually a sign of a lack of self-worth. Excessive love for things may be a sign of inability to love either ourselves or others. Our problems with commitment to God and other people are the same problems we have with being authentically committed to ourselves.

Trying to prove that we can always make it on our own is a part of the sickness of our society. We do not want to be dependent on anyone. But we are dependent upon God and our brothers and sisters, and we will never regain our humanity until we accept this. To the extent we are too proud to ask our brothers and sisters for help, we have cut ourselves off from them.

A good exercise for all of us would be to become a beggar for a while as Francis of Assisi did. If we could see ourselves as beggars we would be more prepared to share. Sharing involves giving, but it also includes allowing others to share with us. It means allowing even the most destitute to share with us.

Sharing is not done out of duty or even primarily to help the other (paternalism), but to commune with the brother or sister and participate with him or her in the new life of the kingdom. Sharing is part of what it means to live in the new age. It is integral to our communion with others and with God. It is an expression of the essence of the new reality. We share not that others might have more, but that all of us might together be what we are meant to be.

Gambling and Lotteries

Since there is an increasing trend toward accepting lotteries and legalized betting, a word should be said on gambling. This can include anything from horse racing and slot machines to playing the stock market. Taking risks in faithfulness to our calling is not included in our understanding of gambling.

Gambling is an expression of the Mammon spirit. It is based on an appeal to selfishness and encourages greed. It is one of the decadent expressions of capitalism. Its philosophy is to get rather than to share. The hope of the gambler is to get the property of one's neighbor by chance.

Chance is the name of the game. Somehow fate, luck, or fortune (pagan concepts) will miraculously change our lives and we will live happily ever after. Gambling is a flight from reality. The Christian, however, depends on God's free grace and love rather than chance. Rather than looking for a lucky break, we can face life with the confidence of God's love and care for us, believing that we will be given the strength to face whatever comes.

Gambling is based on the idea of getting something for nothing, the desire to get rich without working. Neither the desire to get rich or not to work are Christian. There are no short cuts to the good life.

One way we cope with our empty existence is to nurture the hope that some day we will strike it big. It is an opiate to keep us contented with what is, a trick to help us continue to accept the validity of our greedy society. As long as we think we have a chance to make it to the top we will continue to accept the injustices around us.

Gambling destroys people. Gamblers Anonymous estimates there are ten million compulsive gamblers in the United States. Consider all the suffering this creates—the hungry children, the shattered dreams, the broken persons. Gambling exploits especially the poor and perpetuates poverty. It is addictive and leads to slavery.

Perhaps most destructive of all is what happens to the "winners." Suddenly receiving a large sum of money upsets normal patterns of living and often causes disaster, including broken homes, alcoholism, and irresponsibility.

Legalizing gambling may or may not take it out of the hands of organized crime (but let's not doubt their ingenuity). Either way, it still undermines the morals and stability of society. Socialist societies understand this and have outlawed it. A good society is not built on chance or greed, but on relationships of integrity.

Some argue that they play the lottery only in the hope that if they win they can give it all to charity. But even such motivation is based on selfishness—the dream of all the good *I* can do. No matter how worthy the use we intend for it, gambling is based on an attitude opposite to that of sharing, sacrifice, and self-giving. And the argument that the taxes on gambling will pay for schools and welfare is no justification for all the harm it creates. It will never bring prosperity or health to any society. The ends do not justify the means.

Gambling must be seen as a social evil with highly destructive effects for both persons and society. If it cannot be stopped, at least we can refuse to participate in this destructive practice. When people unite in non-cooperation with evil, such practices soon decline.

Clothing

Simplicity relates directly to the question of clothes. How we dress is a fairly good indication of our values. Clothes are symbolic of who we really are as persons. The distinctive dress of the Amish and Hutterites, the Brethren, Mennonites and Quakers of the past expressed many important concerns. The Bible also shows a concern about clothes.

> Let not yours be the outward adorning with braiding of hair, decoration of gold, and wearing of robes, but let it be the hidden person of the heart with the imperishable jewel of a gentle and quiet spirit, which in God's sight is very precious.
>
> *1 Peter 3:3,4.*

Legalistic rules concerning clothes, are obviously not the answer. But how one dresses should be consistent with one's values and life-style. Culture and climate must be taken into consideration. There is a difference between a fur coat for a wealthy, aspiring lady or for an Eskimo. But extravagant clothes and jewelry are not consistent with a liberated life-style. Nor is it appropriate to choose one's clothes to express one's favored rank and position in society.

Clothing should find its proper subordination to the quality of the life we live.

We need not conform our lives to satisfy the dictates of clothing. How often people say, "I can't do that because I don't have the right clothes" or "I'm not dressed well enough to go there." Clothes are made for people, not people for clothes. Fancy clothes inhibit freedom. The person who wears casual clothes can do whatever seems appropriate at the time. We must feel sorry for the man who feels compelled to wear a warm coat on a hot day. If he were not so enslaved to his image and what others think of him, he could be liberated from his burden. Women are just as silly with their high heeled shoes and tight girdles.

Fear of what others may say makes us a slave of their opinions and causes us to do the most ridiculous things. The less concern we have with whether we are properly dressed, the more freedom we can have. The fewer types of clothes we need, the less trouble they are for us. Many people no longer see any need for a big variety of clothes.

Some argue that on these insignificant issues we should conform to society so that when we refuse to conform on important issues we will be heard. Why bring attention to oneself on these insignificant issues? Well, if it is no big issue, why urge people to conform? Apparently to most people it is a big issue. Maybe by dressing comfortably we can witness to the unimportance of clothes. Maybe by wearing a sport shirt on a hot day we can encourage other men to liberate themselves. Those who are unable to take a stand on little things are unlikely to do so on important issues.

We do not need to dress according to acceptable standards of respectability. For example, I refuse to wear a necktie. Not that this is any big issue or that it is evil to wear one, but it is a symbol of the old culture. Since most of the evil in our world is consciously planned and organized by men wearing neckties, this is one small way of saying that I am going in a different direction.

Not dressing according to acceptable standards may symbolize a lack of self-respect or respect for others and this is not healthy. But on the other hand it may be a sign of deep self-respect while conformity to acceptable patterns can be a sign of lack of self-respect and submission to the will of others. (Pseudo hippies who buy expensive clothing tailored to look sloppy and unconventional are missing the whole point, however.)

Simplicity means liberation from slavery to each new advertising campaign. Fads, fashions, and status pass away. Many are slaves to fashion because they fear being "behind the times." They ignore the possibility that the latest fashion may not be in harmony with God's will. Maybe the fashions are "behind the times" since they are a part of the old system that is passing away.

Why should we judge a person's worth and character by the kind of clothes he/she wears? We need new people, not new clothes. If people were more concerned about their souls than their clothes we would all be better off.

Jesus accused some religious leaders of being "like whitewashed tombs, which outwardly appear beautiful, but within they are full of dead men's bones and all uncleanness" (Matthew 23:27). This reminds us of politicians and businessmen who dress immaculately, but whose words and deeds reveal the filth that is in their souls. Having a patch on one's clothes is far better than suffering a guilty conscience for robbing the poor to wear fine clothes.

Dress so that attention is called to your face rather than to the rest of your body. Your clothes should encourage people to relate to you as a person rather than as an object.

A word must be said here regarding obscenity and indecency. Real obscenity is wearing clothes that cost several hundred dollars, gorging oneself while others starve, building oneself a hundred-thousand dollar house. Indecency is a woman with a fifty thousand dollar diamond snuggled between her breasts. Indecency is more than the dehumanizing pictures in *Playboy;* it is also the ads which tell us that to be human is to indulge in more and more of the most expensive and exquisite. A sign of dehumanization is the inability to recognize obscenity and feel indignation toward it.

Jewelry is expensive and only detracts from the beauty of the person. Most jewelry is ugly, poor art, and little more than a collector of dirt. Money spent on trinkets and trash to glorify our bodies debases our humanity. The human body is beautiful as it is. But many are ashamed of their bodies and deform themselves to hide what they hate. Most cosmetics are dehumanizing. Wrinkles in an elderly woman's face are preferable to a face plastered with rouge.

Real beauty lies in the personality, in a pure heart. Rather than being so concerned about outer beauty, one should concentrate on inner beauty. More important than any jewelry or physical adornment is the beauty of love, integrity, openness and faithfulness.

Commitment

Simplicity also involves commitment. To be committed one does not need to be famous or accomplish great feats. Faithfulness in small things is the basis of great achievements. Many are unfaithful not because they are unconcerned about big issues and causes, but because they neglect little things. Those who cannot be trusted in little things can also not be trusted in larger things.

Follow the little light that God has already given you. As you act on the insight you have, more will be given. But do not expect more light until you follow what you have.

Relate first to needs near at hand. Notice what can be done now. Be concerned not only about those far away, but also about the people right in front of you. They are hungry and lonely too. Learn to know the needs of your next-door neighbor. Do not neglect your children for something bigger.

When all of life seems to fall apart, gather together the little fragments that remain and do not discard them. Do not ignore the little experiences and hopes you have had. Keep holding on to that branch even if it is all you have to cling to.

Simple commitment is the deepest commitment of all. Those who are overly involved in many good causes often never really commit themselves to any of them. Serving on thirty committees and attending three committee meetings an evening is not commitment. More likely it is a sign of running from something. Complicating our lives by squandering our energy is not commitment.

Special Occasions

The observance of special occasions can be simple. They are so significant that they should not be ruined by a lot of fuss and bother. The most significant events of life—holidays, weddings, funerals—need not be elaborate. The more elaborate they are, the more distraction there is from the meaning of the occasion.

These occasions tend to become harried times filled with dressmakers, hairdressers, and photographers in addition to the commotion of gifts, flowers, and dinners.

Thoreau's comments challenge us to consider what is important:[3]

> I sat at a table where were rich food and wine in abundance, an obsequious attendance, but sincerity and truth were not; and I went away hungry from the inhospitable board. The hospitality was as cold as the ices. I thought that there was no need of ice to freeze them. They talked to me of the age of the wine and the fame of the vintage; but I thought of an older, a newer, and purer wine, of a more glorious vintage, which they had not got, and could not buy. The style, the house and grounds and "entertainment" pass for nothing with me. I called on the king, but he made me wait in his hall, and conducted himself like a man incapacitated for hospitality. There was a man in my neighborhood who lived in a hollow tree. His manners were truly regal. I should have done better had I called on him.

This is not to deny that certain occasions demand extravagance. There is a time for feasting. We have an extravagant God who lavishes his blessings on us. Extravagant occasions can maintain simplicity and need not oppress us, however. Also, if we usually live frugally we can have more appreciation for occasional extravagance.

Leisure

Leisure is becoming an increasingly serious issue and the future of our society may largely depend on what we do with it. Leisure can be the breeding ground for decadence or it can mean liberation.

Free time assumes freedom. Without being free, one has no free time. In the same way meaningful leisure presupposes meaning and purpose. It can never be experienced simply by killing time. You cannot kill time without damaging eternity. Leisure is free creative activity. We need not only leisure time, but a leisure spirit.

---

[3]Thoreau, *Walden*, pp. 219-220.

The Jewish sabbath recognized the necessity for a creative pause. It was not meant as a time of idleness, but rather a time to remember that God is our creator and sustainer. Recreation means to re-create. It implies renewal and change of pace. Some people put so much effort into having a good time that it is an exhausting endeavor. Why try so hard to enjoy ourselves? Why not just enjoy ourselves? The simple pleasures are usually the most profound. The deepest pleasures cannot be bought or sold.

The best things in life are free. If people did what they enjoy most, what would they do? Play games, hike, work together, make love, get together with other people—all of which cost little or nothing. To mix poetry and humor into our lives is neither costly or exhausting.

The drug of affluence robs us of many of life's deeper pleasures. Jesus said that to enter the good life we must become as little children. Think of all the joys and the pleasures of childhood. Unless we move beyond the frills and artificial pleasures and live simply as children we will never experience the joy of the new age. Joy is innocent, uncomplicated, and simple. Simplicity and pleasure are old friends.

Reflect a moment on the present standards of leisure in our society. Leisure is shockingly maldistributed. Some have much and others none. The standards of leisure are low. Millions participate in sports only as spectators. We have lost the joy of participation. We even have a spectator attitude toward fun. We depend on others to amuse us. And even most of this is of poor quality. Personal pleasure is destroyed to a large degree by commercial exploitation of recreation. Joy, spontaneity, and celebration are replaced by amusements that are empty and sterile. The primary purpose is to make money for the sponsors and help us pass the time, not to provide us with recreation and pleasure. If people discovered the most rewarding kinds of leisure the gross national product would be cut at least 50 percent.

Increasingly, our entertainment and recreation have become mechanized activity subject to business interests. We are told that true happiness lies in snowmobiles, boats, and other expensive equipment. It is another way of trapping us in the consumer economy. In addition to being a big waste, most of these things lead to shallow lives. They are too thing-centered. There are more creative and fulfilling things to do than drive a snowmobile all day.

We have been told that anything really enjoyable is either fattening, immoral, or too expensive. The truth is just the opposite. What is fattening, immoral, and expensive in the long run is really not enjoyable, fulfilling, or satisfying.

A word needs to be said about hobbies. Some are creative and some are not. The idea of collecting and hoarding things should be carefully examined. Often it is a sickness. Take antiques, for example. It is nice to have old things, but no piece of furniture is worth a thousand dollars. Hobbies can result in slavery to things, or they can be creative.

Don't pick a hobby. Simply pursue the things that interest you most. You will discover activities and interests that will fascinate you and give you much free entertainment. And you will end up with a hobby that is your own.

Leisure is important. We need more of it. But leisure implies freedom and we are still slaves. True liberation points us to activities that are creative, enjoyable, and fulfilling.

Work

Work is an important part of what it means to be human. Creative work can bring dignity to our lives. Even menial tasks can provide depth and perspective. Washing dishes can be a meaningful activity if done with the right attitude and if men help. One can work in a garden all day and not feel lonely, bored or oppressed. Work is a great levéller. It can bring people together. Those who do no physical labor live an unbalanced life.

It is important that earning a living be a joyous activity. Forty hours a week is a large chunk of your life. Don't waste it doing something you hate. The process of feeding, clothing, and housing ourselves should be a creative and satisfying activity. Don't be a slave to work. Do what you are called to do and find ways of supporting yourself by doing it. Maybe the perfect job for you does not yet exist and you must go out and create it.

Employment should not be basically to earn money (except when one works a few hours to support the rest of one's service), but to serve the good of all. Vocations are not equally valid. Garbage collection is an honorable profession, but working in a factory producing war materials or junk is not. Our employment should be connected with those things that sustain life rather than death and oppression. Choose not what will make you the most wealthy or respected, but that in which you can do the most good. Seek the most creative and socially helpful job rather than the best paying one.

Shape your life-style so that you are not exploiting others. Do your share of menial labor. Men can share in household duties and women in mechanical jobs. Share the dirty jobs.

Smoking, Drinking, and Drugs

Simplicity also applies to the question of smoking, drinking and drugs. These activities do not fit into the life-style I wish to live. Our lives can be fulfilled and enriched in other ways. Just because these things are widely accepted is no reason why we should use them.

Smoking, drinking, and drugs are moral issues of valid concern. It seems inconsistent to see the Vietnam war as a crucial moral issue but not smoking, even though over two hundred thousand people are killed by smoking in the United States alone each year. In the last ten years over two million people were killed by smoking in one country. Estimates are that in the same ten years we killed about one million people in Vietnam. So these are moral issues and we need to begin to treat them as such. Anything that degrades people or robs them of their humanity is immoral. We should protest all social evils, not just the ones we find convenient.

We will begin by focusing on alcohol since much we will say about that relates also to smoking and drugs. We cannot say that all drinking is evil, but the Bible clearly condemns drunkenness. Although it does not forbid all drinking, it gives many warnings concerning its dangers. "Wine is a mocker, strong drink is raging and whoever is deceived thereby is not wise" (Proverbs 20:1). Alcohol has created many problems and Paul's words seem appropriate. "All things are lawful, but not all things are helpful" (1 Corinthians 10:23).

Alcohol is often thought of as a liberator, something which takes away inhibitions that separate us from other people. Actually alcohol makes one less responsive and hurts authentic communication between people. I much prefer to talk with people when they are not drinking. Drinking erodes the basis of our humanity by weakening the will and reducing self-control. Alcohol tends to bring out the worst in people and has often destroyed relationships. Eating together builds deeper relationships than drinking together.

Alcohol is a crutch rather than a liberator. Often it is an escape, a refusal to accept who we are, and an attempt to be someone we are not. This applies not only to the alcoholic, but also to the social drinker who depends on alcohol to be more "sociable." If we need alcohol to be sociable we should begin to deal with the real problem. Drug addicts use the same argument. There is a difference between liberation and "feeling liberated." We need to learn to live without crutches whenever possible.

It is important to avoid anything that would detract from our ability to respond to God and our brothers and sisters. Anything that hinders us in reaching out to others in love should be avoided.

We now know that alcohol is physically addictive for some people. Many well meaning people have become addicted. We do not know if we or our brother or sister may become an alcoholic. One out of twelve who drink will become an alcoholic. In the light of this, it seems unloving to encourage anyone to start drinking.

The use of alcohol creates tremendous social evils. It has a direct relation to the moral tone of society. It is directly related to automobile accidents and other similar tragedies, marital breakups, alcoholism, poverty, and the increase of aggressive crime. If we personally knew the hell alcohol creates in many lives maybe we would think more clearly about our responsibility toward the problem. In the United States alone, over fifteen billion dollars are spent on alcoholic drinks each year. Between six and ten million people suffer from alcoholism and a much larger number could be classified as problem drinkers. Think of all the dehumanization and suffering this represents!

At least fifty percent of highway deaths are caused by drinking drivers. That means over twenty-five thousand deaths in the United States each year, plus countless injuries. Drinking is responsible for four to six billion dollars in loss of work. A major percentage of all arrests are for drunkenness. Social drinking brings no value equal with the evil it causes. Any value it might bring can be found in other more desirable ways. A good rule to follow is moderation in good things and abstinence in harmful things.

Honesty forces us to admit that alcohol really does not belong in a modern society. It did not create as many problems in primitive times as it does today.

Then there were strong community ties, pressures, and mores to maintain solidarity within the society. But in a society such as ours—already full of despair, hopelessness, and lack of meaning—it is imperative that we encourage people not to start drinking. The dehumanization of the modern world makes addiction more appealing and more difficult to resist.

In primitive society there was no technology which required quick thinking and reactions at all times. Today it is unsafe to go for a walk after drinking. Today the drinks are much stronger and they are pushed upon us by advertising which connects drinking to the fulfillment of deep personal needs. There is a qualitative difference between drinking today and in the past. Alcohol does not belong in a modern society.

The increasing rate of consumption of alcohol cannot be seen as a good sign. It is important that respected people speak up and exert strong influence in this area. Of course, most of society will probably never go along with total abstinence from alcohol just as it will never accept many other important values. Society will go on drinking and we will need to deal the best we can with the tragic consequences. It will probably never agree to give up a little "enjoyment" to avoid major social problems even though this would be a minor sacrifice compared with the advantages.

Christians never should base their morality on the way things are, but begin to live now the way things could and will be, and seek to be completely faithful to God.

It is not enough merely to oppose drunkenness. Almost everyone opposes that. Education on how to drink properly is also of doubtful help. And do not believe all the stories about various ethnic groups not having alcohol problems. European countries are noted for their alcoholism, despite myths to the contrary. Someone needs to say that drinking is not a good thing. Total abstinence is no more irrelevant that total non-cooperation with war. The approach of gradual reform does not seem to get us very far. A more radical witness is needed.

Many preface their arguments to justify drinking with phrases such as: *if* a person never drinks much, *if* it is done in moderation, *if* it causes no harm or injury, *if* it never leads to excess, and so on. But all these ifs are not the reality we face in our world. Almost everyone I know who argues for drinking responsibly will drive an automobile after drinking, even though that is irresponsible. Most of the accidents caused by alcohol are not caused by drunks, but by people who had only a few drinks. The private understanding of morality is not a responsible ethic. We need a social ethic that includes social responsibility.

We need to choose a life-style that points in the direction we want society to move and that expresses the values we hold important. We need to be a people who can have fun without drinking. There are alternative ways to celebrate. Alcohol does not produce joy. Drinking parties are not very joyous or happy occasions. The best parties center around something other than drinking. Life can be fuller than experiencing the deadening effects of the alcohol culture and the sterility of cocktail parties.

Drinking is another manifestation of materialism. Alcohol is expensive and siphons money away from good causes. To drink even moderately gives both moral and financial support to a system and practice that creates great amounts of suffering. Refusing to drink is another way of resisting the oppressive pressures of the consumer society.

If you are not self-righteous about it, you will not lose any friends and will actually gain influence. People will soon know you have integrity and will not be pushed around by anyone. Simply say, "No, I don't care for any, but I'd love something else." Never apologize for your stand.

So much is currently being written about smoking that we need not say much here. The health problems related to it are well documented. For the Christian who takes stewardship of one's body seriously, no position seems possible other than to oppose smoking.

In the past seventy-five years the tobacco industry with its money, experienced advertisers, and sharp psychologists has transformed the United States into a nation of tobacco addicts. Smoking is an excellent example of how a major problem (in this case, health) was deliberately imposed on a society by people pursuing power and profit. Liberation leads one to say no to such crass exploitation.

We have a responsibility to others, especially children. Anyone who knows children realizes how they imitate adults. What is my responsibility to a person who, partly because of deep respect for me, later takes up smoking and dies of cancer? We know that most people take up smoking at the point of their identity crisis.

I appreciate clean, fresh air. But much of my life I am forced to breathe air polluted with smoke blown from the lungs of my brothers and sisters who smoke. A friend of mine has a throat cancer and should not breathe tobacco smoke, but people continue to smoke in his presence. It seems that non-smokers should have as much right to clean air as smokers have to their smoke. Maybe smoking should be prohibited in all indoor public areas to protect the rights of non-smokers. Have you ever thought of how hypocritical it is to sit in a smoke filled room and discuss the evils of air pollution?

And then there are drugs, both the legal ones adults use to cope with society and the illegal ones youth uses to find a new reality. First, to be honest, we must say that much of the use of mind expanding drugs is not as depraved as the alcohol culture. Much of the youth drug culture is a search for spirituality rather than an escape from it. That is more than we can say of many of the legal drugs. But it is becoming increasingly clear that this road is a dead-end street.

Drugs do not lead anywhere. While at first people often get a feeling of new sensitivity, openness, and unity, continued use of drugs usually leads to the opposite results. Drugs have done more to destroy love, joy and spontaneity than develop it. Those who use drugs are following the American way of satisfying emotional and spiritual needs through consumption. The result is that our bodies become machines to be turned on and off.

Drugs are a form of hedonism. Hedonism leads to slavery, not liberation. The use of drugs become a crutch upon which we become dependent for stimulation and pleasure. The continued use of drugs focuses concern on one's private feelings. It makes people self-centered and less able to relate creatively to others. Drugs make one more ingrown rather than more open.

We cannot say that no one has found new insight and sensitivity through drugs, but we can urge people to stop using them, for drugs are not the way to the good life. Drugs do not lead to salvation. This can happen only in relation to God and to other people.

Liberation is in relation to history and is more than personal salvation and mysticism. It seems better to develop a counter culture which will blend internal search and sensitivity with relatedness to others in social struggle. We can develop a new life-style that will be both fulfilling and liberating.

CHAPTER 3

You Have a Good Point, But—

MANY PEOPLE ARE QUITE SYMPATHETIC TO the ideal of simplicity, yet have too many questions and doubts to ever try it themselves. Even those who live simply have their doubts. Here are some common questions with partial answers.

Aren't you trying to turn back the clock and oppose progress?

Actually turning back clocks or setting them ahead is a common act. We can turn back clocks. Maybe what is meant is that we cannot turn back the calendar. That is true. But one need not hold a fatalistic view of history in which our duty is to adjust ourselves to what is, to fate, and the status quo.

For Christians the world has been defatalized. What *is* is not what must be. Christians set their watches not by the times, but by the promise of God for the future. We are living in the new time. Things can be changed. They do not need to be the way they are now. Repentance (turning to the opposite direction) is a possibility. If we can revert to all kinds of barbarity, we can also turn to better styles of living.

The analogy of a clock is not helpful. It is not the question of a clock, but a compass. The issue is not chronology, but direction. And that we can decide. Shall we continue to go in the direction we have been going or does the future call for a new direction? Our critique of affluence is not based on any notion of the good old days, but on a realistic assessment of the past and present with a view toward the future.

Simplicity is not conservative, but radical. We are not retreating, but looking ahead to perceive what is important. Simplification implies leaving things behind and moving to a new future. The inbreaking of the future into our lives makes much of the present irrelevant.

Isn't simplicity an escape? Doesn't it show an unwillingness to deal with the complexities of our modern world? Isn't simplicity a camouflage for irresponsibility and escapism?

It is true that this can be an escape. It can be a search for personal salvation without social involvement. One can get so caught up in growing one's own food and making one's own clothes that one never gets around to making any other contributions.

One can also call it irresponsible to delay living the good, simple life until tomorrow. The way we live now helps shape the future. The means determine the ends. We do not solve our problems by contributing to them and perpetuating them. It is a sad fact that most of us spend a major portion of our lives helping perpetuate the things we say we oppose. In the name of responsibility we continue our support of the old society.

We need a new understanding of responsibility to society. In a society gone mad we need the witness of a new kind of life. In the midst of the absurd, someone must begin to live with meaning and purpose. Instead of symbols like shallow movie stars, power hungry politicians, and greedy capitalists, we need the witness of a Francis of Assisi to call us to sanity.

We have a responsibility to help develop and expand those things (*e.g.* health care) and types of relationships (participatory democracy) that we would want to see in a post-industrial society. We should be working on these now. Responsibility does not lie in perpetuating the status quo or adjusting ourselves to the bureaucratic system, but in starting to develop a new order. We are responsible for living the best life possible in faithfulness to God, to point others to new possibilities.

Simplicity is a break in the chain of complexity. Life does not need to become increasingly more complex. Mark Twain is supposed to have said, "Civilization is a limitless multiplication of unnecessary necessaries." He was right, but it need not be that way. Bondage to necessity can be broken. Necessity is only another word to justify our slavery.

The increasing complexities are not making people happier, more loving, or closer to each other. Our lives become shallow and meaningless through the over-abundance of opportunities and stimulation. Our learning more and more about less and less will produce greater and greater ignorance unless we begin to step aside for a new perspective. We use complexity as an excuse for not reaching conclusions and answers. Lowering the level of complexity will mean raising the level of vitality.

The way to master complexity is not through increasing complexity, but by finding simplicity in the midst of complexity. We need a new simplicity to unite our fragmented world. Simplicity is not an escape from responsibility, but a discovery of a new and deeper responsibility.

Doesn't simplicity mean that those who are living simply are benefiting at the expense of those who work hard within the system?

This question should cause deep humility on the part of those who would simplify. Yes, we are dependent upon all our brothers and sisters, in or out of the system.

That, however, is no argument against simplicity. Rather it is a reminder of how interdependent all of us are. To the extent we recognize our interdependence and share all we have with others we will simplify and move away from individualistic living.

This does not mean that simplicity would be impossible without some persons remaining in the old way of life to support those who choose to live more simply. With a new style of interdependence and sharing, greed and hoarding would not be necessary. Those who live simply and are dependent upon the old system, have not yet developed alternatives to it. One should attempt to be independent of the old system, but never cut oneself off from those still living within it. Being supported by those inside the system should not be a basis for living simply.

Some also object that one is enjoying the benefits of society without contributing to it (e.g. paying taxes). While one may not earn enough to pay much taxes, that in no way means that one is making no contribution to society. What our society needs most is not more money, but the contribution of moral energies. One's contribution can be in non-monetary ways. Those who live simply can and should serve human needs.

Isn't simplicity poor stewardship of time and talent?

It can be, but it need not be. Our first task is to be faithful. If we are faithful our talents can be put to much better use than when we compromise to be effective. Through singleness of purpose we can be most free to respond with our talents to needs.

We should not have an inflated view of our own talents. Others also have talents which can be used. Those who jet across the country for a two-hour meeting have a highly exaggerated view of their own importance. Our stewardship is important, but we must allow others also to exercise stewardship. The powerful would be exercising good stewardship if they shared most of their power and responsibility. Egoism is a poor argument against simplicity.

Simplicity does not mean becoming lazy and lethargic, but focusing activity in a new direction. It does not mean poor stewardship of talents, but putting talents into more positive and creative endeavors. Giving up our affluence may not solve all the ills of society, but not giving it up may well prevent us from solving many of them. Simplicity means liberation of our talents.

Some say one should earn as much as possible to be able to give more to worthy causes. This argument is also fallacious. Commitment is what is most needed. Many jobs compromise if not destroy that commitment. If the commitment is there, the money will come. Jesus made it very clear that the widow who gave the only penny she had gave much more than those who gave out of their abundance. Our total commitment is needed more than all our compromises.

Doesn't simple living add to unemployment? Isn't it better to keep buying luxuries in order to give employment to others? Wouldn't simplicity hurt the poor?

While in the short run the use of luxuries may add to employment, in the long run our luxurious living hurts the poor. Our indulging ourselves so that others can have employment at a much lower level of salary only perpetuates an unhappy situation. Our luxuries take food out of the mouths of the poor. Actually the same argument is often raised against peace and disarmament. This poem, by an anonymous author, unmasks our rationalization.

> Now Dives daily feasted
> And was gorgeously arrayed;
> Not at all because he liked it,
> But because 'twas good for trade.
> That the poor might have more calico,
> He clothed himself with silk;

And surfeited himself on cream
That they might have more milk.
And e'en to show his sympathy
For the deserving poor,
He did no useful work himself
That they might do the more.

The production of luxuries requires unnecessary labor and materials which could be used in other ways. Since our productive capacity is limited, every useless article produced prevents production of necessities. This helps increase the prices of necessities and thus lowers the real wages of the poor and increases their suffering. The production of luxuries, while seemingly providing jobs and income, serves to depress real wages and provide income on jobs that are insecure and the first to be cut off in a recession. The fewer people employed in the production of luxuries the more economically secure the people will be.

Within the context of the old system and its values, simplicity could mean unemployment (as automation also can). If we reorder our priorities, restructure the system to reflect new values, and redefine what employment is, simplicity would not mean unemployment. It is the question of how we use our time and resources. Simplicity would cut down on the market for caviar and women's hats but it would increase the market for cabbage and sturdy clothes. It might put the hairdressers out of business, but health care and measures to save the environment could be extended. Our resources would be used for the needs of all rather than the luxury of some. More people would be usefully employed and fewer paid for what is not useful.

Many persons are so enslaved to work that has no value that they could only welcome liberation to new possibilities. By not forcing them into useless jobs we would be doing them a favor. Certainly we must be creative enough to devise other forms of employment which would be useful and productive.

Wouldn't simple living lead to the collapse of our economic system?

The answer to this is easy. Yes, it would mean the collapse of our economic system. Even to take seriously the command to not covet would destroy our economy. But simplicity implies that we begin now to replace our present economy before it collapses. That way, when it falls, no one will miss it.

Simplicity is indeed incompatible with bureaucracy and huge centralized organizations. It would lead to a post-industrial (not pre-industrial) society. Just as simplicity means radical change in our life-styles, it would also mean radical change in the structures of society. We should welcome those changes. Yes, simplicity would lead to a new economic system.

Aren't possessions important to the development of personality? Doesn't ownership help develop a sense of self-direction and self-control and give the person a feeling of security, independence, and responsibility? Doesn't ownership help develop character?

It is interesting to note that most of the great people of history lived with extreme simplicity. Consider Jesus, Buddha, Confucius, Kagawa, Socrates, Francis of Assisi, Gandhi and many inventors and artists. The more mature a personality becomes, the less significance possessions have. The essence of personality is in relationship with people and is expressed through love, friendship, and creativity.

Things are a part of life and our relation to them is important. They affect our perspective, values, and relationships with people. Not to delight in things is to be ungrateful for the world God has given to us. But we must get beyond the commodity fetish that attaches the ego of each person to the possession and hoarding of things. We must move on to a position of true Christian responsibility for the production, distribution, and consumption of things.

Actually this argument runs counter to the consumer ethic. One of the problems with the consumer society is its disregard of things and the lack of any permanence in relationship to them. The consumer society has produced a loss of identity. We live in a throw-away culture and develop a throw-away mentality. More and more things become disposable. What does it do to our understanding of life and personality when we so quickly become dissatisfied with last year's model? The transience of our relationships with things becomes symbolic of our relationships with people. Minimum involvement becomes a life-style. It would be better to have a few meaningful things than to continually flirt with new things.

Simplicity is the regaining of personhood in· a depersonalized society. It is the refusal to allow impersonal things to become the focus of our lives to the extent that outer things dominate the inner self. Instead of attaching our personhood to things and possessions, we can have an identity separate from possessions. It is important that we know who we are and realize that we belong to God, not to the state or economic system. A clear sense of self-identity leads to simplicity.

Isn't poverty oppressive? Why should anyone romanticize it?

It is something to be avoided. Yes, forced poverty is a dehumanizing condition. Life can be so hard that it crushes the spirit and destroys creativity and initiative. We may not use a critique of affluence as a rationale for keeping the poor in poverty. It is sheer hypocrisy for the rich to talk to the poor of the spiritual blessings of poverty. No attempt is being made here to romanticize the lower classes and the poor. Rather, we are trying to be realistic about how affluence is based on the oppression of the poor.

The real problem of the poor is not poverty, but oppression, degradation, exploitation, and enslavement. Thus they need not just more material goods, but liberation from economic slavery and the birth of a new vision. The real problem is not the unequal distribution of material goods, but the system that perpetuates it. Thus to help poor people out of poverty and into the system only reinforces the system and the problem. The lot of the poor is not eased by introducing them to the slavery of affluence. The call for equal opportunity to strive for the sick goals of our society cannot lead to liberation, but to a new enslavement. The Civil Rights Movement in the 1960's was wrong in some of its goals. Those blacks who reject the idea of being integrated into a sick society are more prophetic. Their message is important also for whites.

Voluntary poverty does not include the problems of forced poverty. Forced poverty creates resentment, frustration, and a desire for things. It is dehumanizing and oppressive. Voluntary poverty is founded on liberation, not enslavement. Voluntary poverty is an expression of joy.

Aren't the poor as materialistic as the rich?

Maybe. But the greater problem lies with the rich. However, it is important not to confuse form with substance. The outward form of poverty may be an expression of necessity rather than liberation from slavery. The poor are also enslaved to their dreams of great wealth and power. Greed runs through all social classes.

One aspect of the oppression of the poor is the propaganda that they need more than they have. They may need more, but they have been convinced by the propaganda and by envy of the more affluent that they need what they do not need. This only further perpetuates their misery. They are systematically locked out of the dreams that are expounded to them everyday.

To a large extent, the rich are responsible for the materialism of the poor.

Lack of wealth does not need to lead to a greater concern for things. It is important, however, that one have a spiritual basis that will give fulfillment without wealth. Without vision, hope, or fulfillment, without spiritual depth, all people are likely to center their attention on things.

Only those who live simply can with any integrity explain to the poor that affluence is not the goal. Only they can point to legitimate goals and talk to the oppressed about nonviolence. We cannot relate to the poor in this way unless we are poor. The more voluntary poverty is practiced by the privileged, the more the advantages of simplicity become a possibility for the poor.

Aren't the frugal also materialistic?

This is possible. Those who live frugally can become so concerned about saving money that money becomes the central fact of their lives. Many have become wealthy through being frugal. If one constantly strives to get to the point where General Motors has no influence on one's life, then it has a phenomenal impact. It becomes the center of one's life. The miser does not live in simplicity.

Not only must we talk of the pride of the rich, but also of the pride of the humble. There is a real danger of pride in wearing old clothes with holes in them. We become proud of our sacrifice and begin to think that we are morally superior to everyone else. Instead of thinking of ourselves as holier than thou we see ourselves as simpler than thou. This self-righteousness can make virtue distasteful.

Yes, the frugal can be as materialistic as the rich. We also can care more about things (or lack of things) than about people. But that is no reason to accept slavery to things.

Won't mass production solve the problem of scarcity? Don't we now have the ability to provide enough goods for everyone and establish more freedom than ever dreamed of? Isn't progress measured by the increase in people's desires and their satisfaction? Isn't simplicity at best an anachronism?

It has not yet happened. Most of the world still lives in poverty. Even in the United States, the richest nation, we are still a long way from ending poverty. The end of unemployment is not in sight. The problem of scarcity has not been solved. In fact, it may be getting worse. The gap between the rich and poor seems to be widening.

The emphasis of technology is on the quantitative rather than the qualitative. However, the crucial questions are moral, not technical. The real growth of civilization is not in increasing affluence, but in the development of relationships. Civilizations cannot be meaningfully built on an unlimited flow of goods.

Some argue that the answer is not in redistributing the wealth, not in cutting the pie in smaller slices, but in enlarging the pie. This must be rejected. It is ecologically irresponsible. It recognizes no need for fundamental change in the system. It fails to recognize the repressiveness of affluence or the fact that it is inherently based on exploitation. This mentality urges spreading the mass consumption society with all its values all over the world. Mass production and consumer affluence are not the answer to the needs of the world.

Isn't it important for the intelligent to be rich? Don't they deserve more? Wouldn't the poor only waste any extras they might acquire?

Aside from being racist, there is no foundation for this argument. A brief glance at history shows how irresponsible the rich have been. This is simply a rationalization used by every ruling class. If we accumulate possessions we may argue that we will use them only for good purposes (highly unlikely, knowing that they were gained and maintained by oppression). Even so, how are we to know that they will not be used for evil purposes after we are gone?

If the poor are irresponsible, it may be because they have never been allowed to be responsible. Who are we to say that they should not have better food, housing, medical care, and education? Who are we to keep from them what belongs to them? Maybe they would be no more responsible than the rich, but that is no reason to maintain the irresponsibility of the rich.

Even if we had the purest of motives (we don't), it would be wrong for us to paternalistically give to the poor. All people need the opportunity to create their own lives and build what they use. No group will long endure the plight of being completely dependent on others.

Doesn't simplicity mean the perpetuation of drudgery? Isn't it important to live as comfortably as possible? Isn't it good that technology protects us from the extremes of temperature, famine, and disease? Can't transportation and communication increase the quality of life? Can't affluence free us from oppressive fears and provide a sense of security and leisure time for the development of human potential?

There is nothing wrong with these things. But we do need to examine the myth that the good life consists of using gadgets to do our nasty work for us so that we will have time for the good life. Consider how hard we work to pay for them and keep them all running. Buying one gadget leads to buying another and yet another. If buying A is good, why not B, and then C, D, E, F, and so on? Where do we stop? The point is that we should draw a line.

There is no need to waste oneself in meaningless work. Menial work, however, is not necessarily meaningless. Washing diapers is meaningful work. But we do not need to do all those menial tasks that have little meaning or purpose.

Rather than produce leisure, things make life more crowded and rushed. The telephone can save us the time of running errands, but contacts soon expand and the telephone breaks into our leisure. The mechanized countries are not noted for their leisurely life-styles. Isn't it interesting that in spite of our T.V. dinners, wash and wear shirts, automatic appliances, and high speed automobiles, we seem to have so little time?

Disease and famine have not been eradicated. Note the increase of degenerative diseases such as cancer, heart disease, and mental disorders. Our security is so limited. Things have not given us what was promised.

Life is not meant to be dreary, but pain and discomfort are a part of growth and creativity. Writing this book is painful. To become completely comfortable is to die. To avoid all suffering and pain would mean the end of creativity. Discomfort is not to be avoided at all costs.

Isn't simplicity monotonous?

The opposite seems to be true. The superfluities and vanities of our consumer society are monotonous. They, not simplicity, dull the zest for life. It is the constant stream of artificialities that causes boredom. It is more enjoyable to own a thirty dollar sofa that the children can jump on than a three hundred dollar one that children can't touch and adults feel guilty for sitting on.

Simplicity does not dull the appetite. One never tires of the basic foods such as bread and rice. It is the continual use of highly flavored foods that dulls the taste buds. They only stimulate the craving for more and make the old monotonous. Those who are living simply do not find life boring. It is those in the rat race who complain of boredom.

Isn't simplicity a denial of beauty?

No the simple can be beautiful. Consider the irresistible beauty of a sunset and how it can at least momentarily simplify our lives. Beauty is simplicity. Isn't there as much beauty in the simple lines of modern architecture as in the elaborateness of Baroque? Simplicity is an expression of more perfect form. The simpler things are, the more their form is expressed. Bauhaus architecture is a good example. There can be beauty in the complex, but complexity is not essential to beauty. Proportion, line, color, contrast, and naturalness are important ingredients of beauty. Clutter detracts from beauty. Even the elegant can be simple.

Simple does not mean ugly just as ornate does not mean beautiful. This is not to say that the simple is always beautiful. The simple can be also ugly. But usually the stylish, gaudy, and ornate are not beautiful. Some of the most beautiful homes are decorated with ordinary things used in a creative way. The beauty of creativity is better than the flair of riches.

Simplicity rejects kitsch, the fake art of carnival souvenirs. Because of a deep appreciation of beauty, the superficial products of mass production are discarded. Instead of sentimental nonsense one looks for the authentic, the natural, and the creative. In the midst of all the ugliness of our society we need the protest of beauty. Amid the gaudiness of abundance how beautiful is the protest of simplicity.

Beauty is to be enjoyed and shared. It is not found through hoarding beautiful objects in our possession. True beauty is not a room decorated so luxuriously that one would feel guilty for touching it.

If we go beyond functional to ethical and aesthetic categories, good takes on the connotation of beautiful. What is good is beautiful. Human artistic expression reaches its peak in the struggle for liberation, but most of the artifacts are designed for oppression. That may be why our society is ugly.

Isn't simplicity a sacrifice for your children? Aren't you hurting them? Aren't you stifling their development?

No. Just as simplicity is the best life for adults, so it is for children. It is no sacrifice to live simply. It is not good for children to be smothered in affluence. We destroy our children by giving them everything they ever ask for and more. People shower their children with an abundance of gadgets and toys, but the children are starved for love. Often things are a substitute for love.

Is the indulgence of affluence and privilege the best atmosphere to raise children? Is insulation from struggle a fair preparation for life? Are we really doing our children a favor by providing them with abundance they never worked for? To shower our children with so many gifts at Christmas time that they never appreciate any of them is not doing them any favor.

It is not good for children to have fancy toys with lights that blink off and on automatically. These spectator toys are fun for about five minutes, but there is little one can do with them other than watch them. Let children play with simple things that require imagination and creativity. Children like to play with the things adults use. Allow them to play with the pots and pans. Include them in what you do. Allow them to invent their own games. It is not a sacrifice for children not to have a T.V. to watch. They will have more time to amuse themselves by using their own talents and playing with other children.

Maybe we should begin to be suspicious of the phrase, "We owe it to our children." Do we really? What do we owe to them other than ourselves? Is our goal to help them adjust to a sick society and succeed in it, or is it to raise healthy children? Many of the things we give our children are more oppressive than liberating for them.

But, the questions continue, how can you make moral choices for your children? To teach them that affluence is desirable is to make moral decisions for them. Better let them decide for themselves if they want to be materialistic. At the point children want more things they should be allowed to choose them. Simplicity can not be forced on them. But they can be asked to earn the money themselves. If children choose to be materialistic, let it be their choice.

Moral issues cannot be avoided. Either way we raise them. But what happens to your children if you live in conflict with your conscience, if you live without integrity? We do not need to spend much time telling our children our values. They can see them demonstrated in our lives by living what we believe. That will give our children the greatest amount of freedom.

But don't we have to provide for the future? Isn't it our responsibility to look out for our own security?

Maybe so, but a more significant question is how that is to be done. Jesus said not to worry about the future.

How much greed and selfishness are disguised as providing for the future. Whose future? Well, *mine*, of course. That is part of our problem. That is part of the insecurity of our world. Peter Maurin, founder of the

Catholic Worker movement, has stated the case creatively in his easy essay, "The Case for Utopia."[1]

> The world would be better off
> If people tried to become better.
> And people would become better
> if they stopped trying to become
> better off.
> For when everybody tries to
> become better off,
> nobody is better off.
> But when everybody tries to
> become better,
> everybody is better off.
> Everybody would be rich
> if nobody tried to become richer.
> And nobody would be poor
> if everybody tried to be poorest.

This means we need to develop new means of providing for ourselves. The old way has proven to be most insecure. New forms of security need to be found. Instead of each person caring only about self, we need communities of sharing and caring. New networks of interdependence can be created. Security will be found only in depending on each other and our God.

The good life is possible. The objections need not stop us.

---

[1] *A Penny a Copy*, eds. Thomas C. Cornell and James H. Forest (New York: Macmillan, 1968), pp. 16-17.

CHAPTER 4

So What's Wrong With Being Rich?

OUR UNDERSTANDING OF RICHES MUST TAKE into account our relationship with the rest of the people in the world and with our environment. By this definition, wealth refers not only to the super rich, but to all people living beyond the level of essential needs. That includes most of us.

Obviously, possessions and material things are not evil in themselves, but in the context of a competitive society in which human worth is determined materially, they indeed do become oppressive. Neither are we saying that the coming of "advanced" civilization has no advantages, but that modern civilization has just as many pitfalls as advantages. To live the good life in this context requires an extra amount of wisdom.

Wealth subverts the good life and the more one has the less free one is. But this should not lead us to compare Henry with George and conclude that since Henry has more than George, therefore Henry must be more materialistic, less free, and more evil than George. No, it could well be that Henry is the more liberated of the two. The point is that the more Henry has, the more he will be controlled by it. We are saying that Henry may be better off if he had less.

Nor are we saying that it is absolutely wrong to have more than others. In many cases it is perfectly fine to possess more if one is willing to share it. A person may own a large house or a good collection of books. If these can be made available to others, they can be put to good use and not be oppressive for anyone.

A person earning twenty thousand dollars per year

should not necessarily refuse to accept it, although one should be uneasy with the idea of earning so much. So large a salary is obviously based on exploitation of others, for not everyone could earn it. But if anyone does earn that much, most of it should be given away to worthy causes rather than spent on oneself. At the least, there should be no further accumulation of wealth.

Some may ask if we are justified in worrying about the overconsumption of others? Certainly, if it oppresses others. But we are also concerned about those oppressed by their own possessions. They too need liberation. We will want to share our joy with them. The problem with wealth is both what it does to our hearts and what it does to other people. Both of these are important. Lot's great mistake was his desire for wealth. That desire led him to Sodom and nearly cost him his life. (See Genesis 13:1-13, 19:15-29.)

Tolstoy tells of a farmer who kept buying more land and expanding his operations. Finally he heard of cheap land among the Bashkirs. He sold all he had, made a long journey to their territory, and arranged a deal with them. For one thousand rubles he could buy all the land he could walk around in one day. The next morning he set out and walked far in one direction and then turned left. He made many detours to include extra areas of good soil. By the time he made his last turn he realized he had gone too far. He ran as fast as possible to get back to the starting point before sunset. Faster and faster he ran and finally staggered and fell across the starting point just as the sun set. He lay there dead. They buried him in a small hole, all the land he needed.

Here are some reasons why one should not be rich. Not all of these comments will apply to you, but most of them probably will. You will likely think of still more reasons why it is better not to live in luxury.

Possessions cause us to become dependent on them. They have addictive power.

After using an electric can opener it seems impossible that one could ever have existed without one. We begin to see luxuries as indispensable and become dependent on what is not necessary. They destroy our independence.

Linus said that having his blanket in the wash is like having one's psychiatrist go away for the weekend. That is our relation to much of our wealth. We think we cannot do without it. To the extent that luxury weakens our ability to abstain, to wait patiently for results, and to sacrifice, it destroys our potential for creative living.

Possessions have the tendency to possess their possessors. People become slaves of their wealth. Things are more easily acquired than gotten rid of. They grow on us, obtain power over us, and become our master. We are reduced to the level of serfs with property as our lord. The term, "the almighty dollar," recognizes the power of money. Much of the striving for wealth is a search for power—power over the future and power over others. But usually that power ends up controlling us. Possessions are like fire. They are good servants but cruel masters.

Pagans make things with their hands and then worship them and commit their lives to them. That is exactly what we have done. We bow down and submit our lives to what we have made and allow those things to have dominion over us. We give up control over our lives for a mess of consumer pottage and become imprisoned by the comfortable web society weaves around us.

To what extent have things become central for us? How important are they in our lives? Remember how easy it is to rationalize and deceive ourselves and pretend they do not control us when they do.

Do things dominate our lives or free us for the activities we want to do? Do they make us more flexible or less? We need to be constantly alert to the tremendous enslaving potential of possessions.

Affluence is the new opiate of the people. Today it is basically not religion that is used to keep people subservient to the system, but consumer affluence.

Modern society has such tremendous potential, through affluence, to provide "satisfaction" that it weakens protest and generates submission. If the natives become restless, give them more consumer goods to content them.

The days of bread and circuses are not past. Many people dare not lose their jobs. To keep from losing them, they suppress their deepest feelings and do what they know is wrong. Many people are so tied to the consumer status system that they are bought off from expressing dissent, affirming and rejecting the dominant values. Consumption has become a means of pacification.

Whole societies can be forced into conservativism and traditionalism through the use of affluence. Affluence creates conformist needs. Although we now have the potential for freedom from fear and want as well as freedom to develop and create as never before, affluence is used to buy off our aspirations. It accomplishes this by providing abundant consumer goods with the threat of taking them away if the person does not remain within the carefully defined limits of the system. Anyone calling for change is considered a heretic and seen as threatening the security and comfort of the people. People are conditioned to reject authentic aspirations for freedom. In this way affluence becomes the new opiate of the people, doing what traditionally religion once was seen to do.

How can one fight an evil system when one lives

comfortably in that system? How can we fight what seems to be the source of our existence? Often dissidents can be appeased by being offered high paying jobs in the system. With a vested interest in the status quo one is less likely to want to change it. Often when people become more affluent, they lower their ideals. When the Hebrews on their journey to the promised land remembered the "good life" back in Egypt, they wanted to return to slavery (Numbers 11:4-6). Historically, as the church increased in wealth it lost its soul. Today labor unions become reactionary as they seek higher wages rather than social change. We cannot be serious about changing the system as long as we accept the privileges that are used to keep us pacified and controlled, even while we politely dissent.

We need to be somewhat skeptical (for their own good if nothing else) of those who receive huge honorariums for radical, anti-establishment speeches. There is enough weakness in all of us to know that this must be a real temptation. As we reap more of the "benefits" of the system we are more likely to be taken in by its values.

Luxury is an anesthetic. It deadens us to both our own aspirations and to the concerns of others. It has a fantastic effect on one's consciousness. Affluence changes values and commitments. It weakens the will to resist. The spirit seems to shrivel in a life of ease and comfort. Luxury leads to sluggishness and complacency. It makes us soft. The spiritual giants of history led simple and humble lives. If they had lived in affluence in the midst of poverty they would not have been great. We should comfort the afflicted and afflict the comfortable rather than pander to the notions of the well-to-do. All of us need to be stirred from our slumber.

Wealth does not satisfy. Gaining new possessions stimulates the desire for still more.

Since most of us cannot have all the luxuries of our society, it takes a long time to realize that even if we had them all, our lives would still be empty. Affluence diverts us from what does satisfy. The search for wealth seldom brings its intended results. Striving for power, status, and prestige leads not to fulfillment, but frustration. Hoarding and collecting quickly become compulsions. The bigger the better. The more the greater. More, more, more! Mine, mine, mine!

Most of the affluent refuse to recognize how affluent they actually are. They complain about high prices, taxes, and debts, and explain that others have much more than they. Consider the executive who is receiving over twenty-five thousand dollars a year, but cannot seem to get by on it. This should not only be seen as the height of ingratitude, but as also a profound critique on affluence. A large salary does not satisfy.

Why should we want to satisfy all our desires? Satisfaction seldom equals anticipation. Why rob ourselves of anticipation? Satisfaction in most things decreases with each repetition. Our desires are seemingly boundless and can never be satisfied. Consider the answer of the hermit who, when encouraged to eat a banana for the first time, replied, "No, thanks, I already have more desires than I can satisfy."

It is interesting to compare the stereotype of the nineteenth century capitalists with that of his twentieth century counterpart. The former was fat, gorged himself with food, and tried to satisfy all his desires. The twentieth century capitalist is thought of as more rational. He is not fat, limits his eating, and has disciplined his life so that all his energy is directed into consciously chosen pursuits. Although he proclaims the value of unlimited consumption, he has at least learned that there is a limit to the amount of food one should consume.

There is a limit to what one person can possess and genuinely enjoy during a lifetime. It is ridiculous to talk of unlimited consumption. In the same way that eating too much is harmful to the body, so there is a limit to the amount of possessions a person can use and possess and remain healthy.

Materialism is a diversion. Affluence distracts us from the more important aspects of life, from seeking first God's kingdom.

Maintaining a high standard of living takes so much time, effort, and money from the creative things we could be doing. Consumption is a minor gratification which diminishes the deeper joys such as creativity, sharing, and loving. The more one has, the more difficult it is to live with abandon and spontaneity. When consumption becomes an end in itself, it not only places too high a value on things, but limits our ability to see the relationship of things to higher purposes.

What a tragedy to waste life, to live in vain, to miss the mark. Jesus asked, "What does it profit a man, to gain the whole world and forfeit his life?" (Mark 8:36). Making money is such a minor goal in life that little effort should be put into it. Those who understand what life is all about are not interested in earning a lot of money. The accumulation of wealth is not the aim of a sane person.

To put our major effort into secondary goals keeps us from concentrating on that which should be primary in our lives. It distorts our vision. The result is putting more emphasis on values like punctuality, efficiency, and status than on honesty, caring, and sharing. We become blinded to many other dimensions of life and deprive ourselves of experiences cherished as most important throughout history. The "need" for a large income prevents some from entering vocations they would prefer. Consider the great sacrifices that are made each day. For a few extra pieces of silver (actually copper) we are willing to sacrifice sharing with children and family. We become too busy to read good books and develop deeper friendships. We sacrifice our freedom, our integrity, and even our future. Jesus was right when he said that we cannot live by bread alone. If our path is too well lighted we cannot see the stars.

Many people after obtaining the necessities of life put most of the rest of their energy into striving for more luxury, wealth, and status. Commuters actually spend several hours each day in an automobile, slaves of the auto, their jobs, and suburban homes. At the end of the week there is little left to show for the sacrifice except tired backs and empty hearts. We do not burn our candle at both ends; we cut it in pieces and burn it at many ends.

We postpone the good life and spend the best part of our lives doing what we hate in order to someday have enough money to "enjoy" all those "good things" society has to offer to us. Many people postpone living till retirement and then find those years empty also. Why ride along with our society when the trip is boring and the end of the road offers little that is worthwhile?

A whole society can be diverted from the good life. Instead of all the junk we produce, why not spend more on those things which would actually benefit society? Suppose we got rid of all non-essential production and factories. Not only would we eliminate much dreary labor, ugliness, and misery, but we could put that much more effort into important activities. We could have five times as many medical personnel and teachers as we have now.

Our hunger should be for righteousness, truth, and justice rather than wealth. But we have been diverted from the good life.

Conspicuous consumption distracts because it becomes a substitute for deeper things. Furthermore, it substantially changes the very essence of consuming. To eat food is a basic human need and pleasure, but to eat as a substitute for love or meaning completely changes the nature of eating. Our consumer society drastically changes our relation even to things. The advertising people tell us to buy an automobile not as a means of transportation, but as a diffuse sexual pleasure. We are to buy a certain brand of clothes to achieve a certain character. Such exploitation of elemental human drives is evidence of a deep sickness in our society.

Affluence makes us forget God. It leads to neglect of the spiritual by absorbing the energies of the spirit and hardening our hearts.

The pursuit of wealth deadens our sensitivity to the will of God and our readiness to respond to him. It causes us to turn down an invitation to the feast of life because we bought a field. (See Luke 14:16-24). Things begin to stand in the way of faithfulness.

Possessions destroy faith in God. When we are obsessed with gaining wealth or status, what time do we have to consider our eternal destiny, our relation to the transcendent? Daily affairs become more important. Possessions divert us from the vital source of life and meaning. The mundane supersedes the ultimate. Our lives and passion for the kingdom are deadened.

Wealth raises the problem of allegiance and loyalties. Where our treasure is, there will our heart be also. We cannot serve two masters. That means our possessions soon begin to rival God. We see ourselves in terms of our possessions. It is difficult not to identify ourselves with the institutions which made us rich. They become part of who we are. No longer are we primarily God's children or human beings, but possessors, consumers, landlords, or investors. Our loyalties become attached to what we have instead of to God. Wealth is a hindrance to spiritual development and devotion to money is fatal. The problem with worshiping false gods is that they always let us down because they are not big enough.

Wealth is based on a search for power and stimulates the desire for more power. It is a thirst for power over the future, the opposite of faith in God. The philosophy of wealth is that possessions can bring the future under my control so that I can buy my way through any eventuality. The search for wealth is a denial of God. The biblical warning applies to us.

> Take heed . . . lest, when you have eaten and are full, and have built goodly houses and live in them, and when your herds and flocks multiply, and your silver and gold is multiplied, and all that you have is multiplied, then your heart be lifted up, and you forget the Lord your God . . . and . . . you say in your heart, "My power and the might of my hand have gotten me this wealth." *Deuteronomy 8:11-17.*

Whenever groups become affluent they soon lose their faith and vision and forget God.

Wealth creates an illusion of security.

People desire security and believe it can be obtained through possessions, power, and status. People begin to think that if they have enough, nothing can go wrong. Because of insurance policies, bonds, and land, they need not worry about tomorrow.

Actually it is futile to try to get rich. You lose it all when you die and you are in danger of losing it at any time. It may be stolen or the banks might close. There is not much point in trying to secure our future or in being anxious about it.

Security is not based on wealth. In fact wealth leads to insecurity and fear. Affluence leads to buying bigger locks for our doors, not increased feelings of security. The compulsive worry about what we are to eat or wear is not lessened by affluence, although it may be changed by it. All the wealth of the United States has not made it the most secure nation on earth. Jesus told a story of a man who tore down and built bigger barns and then thought he could live in total security. Jesus said he was a fool. That very night it all fell apart and he was faced with only his own life before God. (See Luke 12:16-21).

More important than earning money is earning people's trust. If people trust you for your honesty, courage, commitment, and willingness to work, you will not need to worry about money. It will be there. Actually money is in itself worthless. Its worth is in its being a symbol of trust. When the trust is gone, the paper money will be worthless. Should an economic crisis come and destroy the value of money, the trust you have earned will continue. Work for the reality, not the symbol.

Many people know of no other way to find security except through affluence. They know of no alternatives to the present system and so believe that security comes with a college degree, life insurance, and bank accounts and consider anything less to be false security. Let's examine life insurance. First it is expensive and a poor investment. Higher income people do not buy it. We need to be aware of what the money is invested in. Do we want dividends and personal security at the expense of war, consumer waste, and other forms of evil and oppression?

Consider also the effects of receiving large insurance settlements. Studies have shown this to be devastating for many families. Often it leads to a drastic change of life-style and values, and sometimes to personal disaster. Frequently the money is quickly squandered.

Life insurance is a way of denying the reality of death. It is better for my wife and children to recognize now that one day they may have to carry on without me. This is one way for me to recognize her liberation and competence. If she received a large payment at my death, she might experience a false security and our friends might think she was well cared for and had no needs. Better insurance is trust in God, close relationships within a community of faith, and confidence that the survivors can carry on. True security is found only in relation to other people and to God, not in things.

Wealth encourages false values. As affluence affects consciousness, it transforms and perverts values and standards.

When we become wealthy, we are tempted to think we have achieved something, when actually nothing of significance has been accomplished. Wealth encourages laziness, vanity, arrogance, and paternalism rather than creativity, love, humility, and fraternity.

Wealth not only encourages greed, but is based on it. Is it not perverse and obscene to buy a diamond necklace for a thousand dollars or to build a hundred thousand dollar house? Yet people's values become so distorted that in a world of starving children they actually buy such things.

Wealth encourages selfishness. It supports the gratification of personal desires and encourages people to turn inward, rather than outward to their neighbors. Wealth perpetuates the distinction between mine and thine. John Woolman, the colonial American Quaker, asked if even the desire to give an inheritance to our children is not really a selfish desire on our part and not in the interest of others.[1]

Did man possess as much land as would suffice for twenty industrious frugal people, and supposing that being the lawful heir to it, he intended to give this great estate to his children; yet if he found on research into the title that one half of this estate was the un-

---

[1]*The Journal of John Woolman* and *A Plea for the Poor*, The John Greenleaf Whittier Edition (New York: Corinth Books, 1961), p. 234.

doubted right of a number of poor orphans, who as to virtue and understanding appeared to him as hopeful as his own children, the discovery would give an opportunity to consider whether he was attached to any interest distinct from the interest of those orphans.

Wealth encourages pride. It tends to make people haughty, snobbish, and arrogant. Hunger for food has never driven people to such depravity as pride has. All our vanity and pompousness is garbage. Pity the person who tries to be great and profound. That person is shallow. Simplicity is the opposite of pride. It is liberation from egoism.

Wealth tends to prevent a poverty of spirit before God. "Blessed are the poor in spirit" becomes a troublesome idea, for to be poor in spirit means to give up even the illusion of all *I* have accomplished. When one becomes wealthy, one begins to think "*I* have earned this: *I* have accomplished this. These things are *mine*." The rich develop a false sense of self-reliance. They forget how they got what they have through the labor of others, how dependent they really are on others. The affluent talk about the poor as if the rich have earned their wealth by themselves.

Wealth leads to valuing things above people. As property becomes more important to us, we lower the value of human life. We step on others both to acquire and to keep what we have. The logical conclusion of this mentality is for the mayors of some of our cities to order looters shot on sight, for obviously property is much more significant to us than human life. Better kill the looter than lose the television set. Destruction of property (even if it is only draft files) is considered much worse than destruction of human life. Some people during the war in Vietnam were more concerned about burning flags and draft cards than burning little children with napalm. That is how perverted we are. Some military strategists justify the use of chemical weaponry because it would *only kill* the people without destroying any property. That is considered a great advance. If your house is on fire would you not go in first to save a child before the Rembrandt painting on the wall? The reality of our situation is that the house is on fire and we are trying to save the trinkets, forgetting both the child and the painting.

Affluence leads to judging a person's worth on the basis of wealth. We consider the wealthy to be of more worth than the poor and so treat them with greater respect. Those who own much are considered important. Rather than measuring people by the integrity of their character, the values they live by, or their ability to love and share, we use the standards of worldly success. In a materialistic society the worth of other people is measured in monetary terms. Even personality and talent are thought of primarily in terms of dollars and cents. Our concern is with how much a person can produce or earn. Rather than people having intrinsic value and money value only as we give value to it, we see money having the intrinsic value and people as much value as money brings to them.

This leads to racist attitudes toward the poor. We consider them ignorant, stupid, and inferior. They are poor because they are inferior. Since private property is the basis of being human, only those with private property are really human. And the more they have, the more civilized they are. The poor are now no longer considered Christ's brothers and sisters, but rather as lazy, shiftless failures.

We have taken it still one step further. Possessions become a measure of a person's moral achievement. We have accepted the idea that to be poor is sin. For some, having wealth is a test of being a good Christian. Because the poor are seen as sinful, the wealthy consider it their duty to restrain the poor. This is done both by oppressing the poor at home and through our external imperialistic ventures. We use even the suffering of the poor to justify their exploitation.

Wealth creates barriers between people. Money and private property separate us from our brothers and sisters and destroy a sense of community among people when some have more than others.

Concentrations of wealth create resentment, envy, and mistrust. They create a sense of superiority among the rich and a sense of inferiority among the poor. How is deep fellowship and sense of community possible between one who lives in luxury and one who is in dire need? The separation of people into economic classes does not make for meaningful relationships, even within those classes.

Affluence leads to artificial relationships with people. It leads to the cocktail parties where men boast of their accomplishments and women compare their dresses. Our consumer society has not brought us together. It has created impersonal supermarkets, but no sense of community. Materialism destroys human relationships and drains them of their vitality. Relationships based on affluence are empty. The pursuit of wealth with all its selfishness and egoism runs directly counter to meaningful social relationships.

Wealth separates us from the poor. It is difficult to identify with the poor because we simply do not understand or even know the problems they face. We can identify more easily with the problems of the President than with the agonies of the peasants in Southeast Asia. We more easily comprehend the anxieties of a businessman than the fears of the poor in our cities. Wealth prevents us from even knowing how they feel. The United States in all its affluence is almost completely alienated from the poor nations.

If I am wealthy, I will hesitate to invite the poor into my home. I may find their appearance revolting. I may be afraid their dirty clothes will soil my fine furniture. I am afraid they might steal some of my valuable art collection or tell someone else who will then rob me. I would feel uncomfortable (guilty?) with them lest the great contrast between our positions would make them feel uneasy or even envious and bitter. Seeing my wealth would only make their suffering more unbearable. I had better not invite them. Indeed, this is what has happened to our larger society and to many of us too.

Until we are willing to identify and stand with the poor and oppressed, all our talk about justice is sheer hypocrisy. One can measure the stature of a society by the way it treats its poorest members. No longer may our words identify us with the oppressed and our lifestyle with the oppressors. We privileged people are a major source of the problem and that problem will not be solved before we give up our privileged position in the world. Actually, it is no privilege at all. We only need give up our slavery which oppresses others.

Our affluence dulls social insights and prevents us from joining the struggle for liberation and justice. When the prophet Ezekiel placed his fortune with the exiles in Babylon and sat with them, the world looked different to him. To live simply makes us more sensitive to the injustices around us, more aware of how others are treated.

Young Albert Schweitzer once wrestled with a schoolmate. After Schweitzer pinned his friend, the lad exclaimed, "If I got broth twice a week as you do, I should be as strong as you are." Schweitzer says of this incident: "From that time on broth became nauseous to.me." This was one of the influences which led him to identify with the poor.[2]

One cannot be wealthy without stealing from others. If everyone possessed only what was needed, no one would be in poverty.

---

[2]Told by Daniel Johnson Fleming, *Ventures in Simpler Living* (New York: International Missionary Council, 1933), pp. 88-89.

If we possess something we do not need we are stealing it from those who do need it. That stealing may be direct or indirect, or it may be only the refusal to share what we have with our brothers and sisters in need. There is a limited amount of resources and wealth in the world. Thus for some people to hoard is to keep things from others. That means that as long as I have more than I need while my brothers and sisters have less than they need, I am stealing from them. The existence of need anywhere means a moral claim on the wealth I have. If possessions are grossly unequal it is necessary that some people not have the full benefits of their own labor. That is theft.

Money and resources wasted are essential items stolen from the poor and from good causes. There can be no justice for all as long as anyone consumes more than is necessary. Simple living is one ingredient needed to establish justice.

The making of luxuries for ourselves diverts energy from production and services which would benefit the poor and less privileged. Where will the money and resources come from to pay for the real needs of society? Obviously it must come from the segments of our economy where most of the money is now spent, namely consumer goods and war materials. There is a relationship between the availability of electric can openers and the shortage of health care. Luxury is theft.

My luxuries are not as important as other's necessities. There is nothing wrong with good food and comfortable living rooms, but when millions have little to eat and barely a place to sleep while we live in luxury we are not being responsible. It is not necessary that our happiness and comfort be paid for by the suffering and death of others. We can find a new understanding of joy and comfort that is not based on oppression.

To build up wealth necessarily involves exploitation, for it is impossible to acquire a fortune solely by one's own effort. For us to become rich, others need to work and live on a standard below our own. Consider the hardships people have to endure so that we can live luxuriously—the rape and slaughter of the Indians and blacks, the oppression of people in the Third World. Think of the assembly lines, the suffering masses crowded into our cities, the pollution not only of our soil but also our soul. In order for us to enjoy cheap bananas we force (with the help of our military) peasants in Latin America to work at extremely low wages. Our affluence is based on our collective theft from people around the world and here at home. Our wealth has dehumanized not only ourselves, but others as well.

Wealth makes us fearful and defensive. Our inner selves become so entangled with our possessions that any attack on them is considered an attack upon us.

Our guilt makes us defensive about what we have. And our fear of losing our wealth causes us to feel the need of defending it. When a person is attached to things, the loss of those things is threatening. Wealth makes us reactionary.

Simplicity can mean liberation from fear. My family is gone from our apartment for long periods of time but we have no worries about our possessions. It is liberating not to need to worry about thieves breaking in and stealing what we have, for we have little worth stealing. If we had fifty thousand dollars worth of jewels in our apartment we would constantly worry about them, probably buy more secure locks, and generally change our attitude.

I will never forget working one summer in Chicago in the Civil Rights Movement. I walked the streets alone at midnight without fear. I had little to lose. But one day I picked up some plane tickets and suddenly became fearful to walk the streets in the daytime. I kept my car locked and looked suspiciously at everyone. Afterwards I was shocked at my reaction. Wealth can do that to us. Wealth causes fear.

Whenever we call something our own that is not a part of our body we get into trouble. We become defensive, exclusive and closed to our brothers and sisters. How much suffering has occurred because people have said, "This is mine, not yours"? To call something our own that is not really ours brings great suffering and grief. To take the selfish route cuts us off from our neighbors, from deeper possibilities for sharing.

We elaborately defend what we have. We build more secure locks and field powerful armies to protect us. The result is that our defensiveness separates us from the human community. We become so convinced of the necessity of protecting our standard of living and vast system of investments that we are ready to sell ourselves and our children to slavery and death to defend it.

Part of the reason we want to police the world is to protect and secure our overconsumption in comparison with the rest of the world. A basic argument for the arms race has been to defend our standard of living from those who want to take it from us. We are prepared to use unlimited amounts of violence to preserve our affluence. An incredibly complex and expensive military system is necessary to assure our continued rape of the rest of the world.

Excessive wealth and inequality are basic causes of the violence in our world today.

It takes little observation to note that it is the wealthy who are committing most of that violence to protect their interests. The very existence of hoarded wealth implies violence. We rely on police to defend it, for it is difficult to defend wealth with truth. Only what is legitimate can be defended with truth and nonviolence. There is something wrong with possession if I need a gun to guard it.

The American standard of living is a basic cause of violence. It is based on imperialism and exploitation, on pushing down the poor for the sake of profit. We enjoy our "privilege" and luxury to a large extent because of the bullet in the revolver of the police who force the dispossessed to stay in their place. The wretched of the earth are forced to do our dirty work for us at meager wages. We have become parasites living on the guts of our brothers and sisters.

Wealth creates resentment and envy which can lead to violence. Excessive differences in standards of living are being challenged by the poor in every part of the world and will no longer be tolerated. If the wealthy look upon their affluence as a right, the poor will regard their outrage as justice. Violence results from frustration of justice. Unless we begin to put a ceiling on our desires, someone else will do it for us. If we do not voluntarily choose to live more simply others will force it upon us.

Economic greed and lust for power, an unlimited desire to possess a limited amount of wealth, leads to violence and war. The more desires and wants we have the more likely we will come in conflict with others. The less just those desires are, the more bitter the conflicts will be. If we oppose the violence of war, how can we participate in the violence of affluence? John Woolman put it well.[3]

> O that we who declare against wars, and acknowledge our trust to be in God only, may walk in the light, and therein examine our foundation and motives in holding great estates! May we look upon our treasures, the furniture of our houses, and our garments, and try whether the seeds of war have nourished in these our possessions. Holding treasures in the self pleasing spirit is a strong plant, the fruit whereof ripens fast.

---

[3]John Woolman, *op. cit.*, p. 241.

Violence takes many economic forms. It is the theft of excessive wealth, the exploitation of overconsumption. It is financial investment in violent institutions such as war industries and employment in unnecessary or violent professions. The more one earns the more taxes one pays to murder people around the world. Violence is an integral part of our economic life.

To a large extent the everyday robberies and stealing are a result of our refusal to live simply. These develop out of the inequalities of our society and are encouraged by the materialistic propaganda which teaches people that material goods are more important than anything else. To acquire becomes imperative. Wealth causes violence.

Affluence causes pollution. Our ecological crisis is a direct result of the way we live.

We ruthlessly conquer the earth in our drive for power and pleasure. Ecologists are telling us that unless our pillage of the earth is stopped immediately, the human race will become extinct. That means us. Not only is the simple life the good life, but increasingly it may be the only life we can live. Our affluence is destroying us in more ways than one.

We simply cannot continue our high rate of consumption. The more we consume, the more we pollute, both through waste and the process of production. It is estimated that the average\American throws away five pounds of garbage every day. In 1969 the United States produced 4,340 million tons of solid waste. That is a huge pile of garbage! Twenty five million pounds of aluminum toothpaste tubes are discarded each year. Fifty thousand abandoned automobiles were towed from New York City streets in one recent year alone! All this is a result of conspicuous consumption.

Not only are waste and pollution a problem, but we

are beginning to realize that the earth does not have
an unlimited amount of resources.[4] Many of our resources are nearing depletion. The United States, with
only six percent of the world's population consumes
over half of the world's goods. Obviously the solution
to the world's problems is not in raising the standard
of living in other nations to our own. We do not even
have the resources to continue supporting ourselves at
the present rate.

It is now clear that Americans must immediately
and drastically reduce their rate of consumption. The
Gross National Product must be cut rather than ex-
panded. Those who talk of increasing production are
irresponsible. We can de-develop our economy by
minimizing production, recycling, and eliminating
planned obsolescence. A life of greatly reduced material expectations is rapidly becoming essential for survival. If we refuse to do it voluntarily, we will be
forced to do it.

Certain animals thrived before the Ice Age, but dis-
appeared because they were unable to change and
adapt to new conditions. Unless we are flexible
enough to change, our fate may be the same.

One of the beauties of simplicity is that human resources are never used up. In fact, the more we use
them the more they develop. The opposite is true of
natural resources. Why deplete our natural resources
and allow our human resources to stagnate?

Ecology is a diversion from the important issues
only in so far as it is seen as a separate issue. But when
seen as intricately related to consumer capitalism, it
becomes a radical issue. When consumerism is seen as
slavery, the focus on ecology can be the beginning of
our liberation.

---

[4]Donella H. Meadows, ed. *The Limits to Growth* (New York:
Universe Books, 1972).

CHAPTER 5

Technology, Capitalism, and the Consumer Society

A CIVILIZATION CANNOT LONG ENDURE ON A materialistic basis. The two civilizations that have lasted the longest, the Chinese and East Indian, both had simplicity as an important characteristic.

We need a thorough critique of the system under which we live, examining the growing power of the state, the forces of production and consumption, and the autonomous nature of technology. Many still look on the problems of our society as minor flaws in a basically healthy social structure.

Ever since Franklin Roosevelt, the United States has been promoting the myth of humanitarian liberalism while at the same time increasing its exploitation of the Third World, expanding the destructiveness of our consumer society, and threatening the world with annihilation. A radical critique recognizes that our problems are symptoms of a deeper sickness in our society. Our society is not suffering from a few superficial problems; it is basically sick. It is a society that produces napalm and pollution.

Liberals assume that society will progressively become better as people work within the established channels to bring about reforms. The present system can solve our problems if given a chance, they say, and if enough good people are willing to get involved and work for change.

Radicals consider this kind of reasoning naive. The problem is at least partly the structure itself. The present institutional framework of society is destructive to basic religious values. It forces good people into oppressive roles. We need to bring together communities

112

of people with a new self-identity who stand over against existing structures, confronting the system both with its failure and with new possibilities and alternatives.

Although our focus is consumer capitalism, most of what is said here will apply just as well to Russian-style communism. The power of the state, the domination of technology, and subordination of people to the forces of production are problems there as well as here. Our primary concern here is with American society, however.

We cannot approach economic problems with absolute answers, but we can bring a unique perspective to them. Our starting point is not the problems we face, but rather the faith which we bring to the situation. Often our trouble is in asking the wrong questions. Our faith can lead us to new questions, even questions that are unthinkable for most of society.

The call of the Christian is not to create a Christian society or solve the world's problems, but to begin living a new life. What is needed is not new programs for economic change which will be imposed from the top down, but people who are willing to change their lives and experiment with new ways of living. The political and economic results of such efforts cannot be predicted. But we believe that God can use our faithfulness.

I confess that I am not an economist and that I am more interested in the moral issues than economic ones. Hopefully economists will go beyond what is presented here and work out the concrete economic implications of new values. Most economists accept the pagan assumptions of our materialistic society and thus reach conclusions based on those values. We need economists who will use other presuppositions and come to new conclusions.

We need whole new concepts of what economics is all about. The idea of getting rich or making money is a perverted view. The focus of economic activity should not be money, but creating a livelihood, sustaining life, and teaching cooperation. One can never live on money. What we live on is food and other necessities. The purpose of economic activity is to provide these for everyone.

The Christian is open to the new. Our world is not the closed world of the technocrats, a world in which nothing new is expected. Because of society's denial of the transcendent it has difficulty accepting anything new or any criticism from outside its own system. The most that can be accepted is different variations on the same theme.

From a Christian perspective, however, all culture, all technology, all that is comes under the judgment of God and can be criticized. They are not autonomous. And so we take a critical look at what is.

We begin by examining the success ethic.

We are told that if a thing works it is good; if it does not work it is not good. Big is better than little; more is better than less. We choose machinery primarily on the basis of efficiency for the capital owner, not human values. We have an instrumental view of values and people. Accomplishing an end is more important than the effect it may have on people or on ecology.

These values of the business world are consciously and unconsciously applied to every area of life. Even the church thinks in terms of size of congregation, budget, and program. Efficiency as a goal should be tolerated only in a few special areas such as health care.

Over against the success ethic stands the One who was crucified. The prophet Isaiah pictured the Liberator as

despised and rejected by men;
a man of sorrows, and acquainted with grief;

and as one from whom men hide their faces
he was despised, and we esteemed him not.
Isaiah 53:3.

Jesus said, "Woe to you, when all men speak well of you, for so their fathers did to the false prophets" (Luke 6:26). "Whoever would be great among you must be your servant" (Mark 10:43). Success is not a legitimate goal. The good is not always successful and what is successful is not always good.

We need a transvaluation of values. The direct opposites of many of the dominant values of our society are much closer to Christian values. Instead of status, pride, wealth, fame, position, strength, and power, we need humility, simplicity, service, integrity, and sharing.

True success is basically the opposite of what society admires. The Bible repeats this theme many times. "The Lord of hosts has purposed it, to defile the pride of all glory, to dishonor all the honored of the earth" (Isaiah 23:9). True success is only that which points to His coming kingdom.

People are becoming increasingly aware that technology has led to the manipulation and domination of both nature and people.

A developing totalitarian complex of technology and militarism threatens either to destroy us or dehumanize us with the artifacts of impersonal existence.

Our runaway technology is creating an inhuman future. It seems to destroy everything in its path, be it landscape, people, tradition, or social institutions. The imperialism of technology knows no natural or ideological boundaries.

Technology has not meant liberation.[1] We live in

---

[1] For a very thorough and perceptive analysis of technology, see Jacques Ellul, *The Technological Society*, trans. John Wilkinson (New York: Vintage Books, 1964).

the most repressive of all eras. People in the past were oppressed by hunger, slavery, and many restrictions, but there was always a part of their lives free for individual thought and action. Modern civilization has found the means to dominate the whole person, even one's secret thoughts. Through the use of technology even the subconscious can be manipulated.

Technology as we know it today implies a whole set of assumptions and values. It has become a world view which assumes that all problems are technical and that anything technology cannot deal with is insignificant. Since the good life can be created by technical means, what is needed is better programs and better management.

Even many church officials have accepted the consultant mentality and bring in efficiency experts to tell them how to run the church better. We think we have figured out the basic issues and only need to find better techniques to solve them. Controversy is considered a sign of lack of communication and understanding, never due to substantive disagreement.

With the coming of modern technology has come the deification of technique. How something is done is more important than what is done or why. We devise ingenious and efficient means to arrive at an insignificant end. Education has been reduced to the accumulation of facts (which will be useful for the functioning of the system) rather than being a search for truth and wisdom.

Even food has been transformed from a natural, tasty treat into an artificial product with a standardized taste. We seem to have a law which reads: Never allow to occur naturally what can be produced artificially. Whatever can be mechanized we think should be mechanized.

We have allowed even the most intimate human relationships to be defined by technological values. Masters and Johnson have become world authorities on sex because they worked with sexual activity as technicians. Technique rather than relationship becomes the focux of sexual relations. Sex, a profound, sacred relationship is reduced to a mechanical activity. Marriage is changed from a covenantal relationship to a contract based on mutual convenience. To argue for casual sex without commitment is to accept the logical conclusions of the technocratic worldview.

To the extent we allow technological and mechanistic values to replace the spiritual, transcendent, and mystical, we allow ourselves to be dehumanized and dominated by technology.

Modern sports are a product of our mechanized society. They are performed with time clocks, elaborate equipment, exact timing, and efficient organization and control. The performer is turned into a machine with actions and movements carefully controlled and mechanized. Breaking records, winning, and efficiency are the goals. This is a technical undertaking much different than play. How different from jumping, playing, or running for the sheer fun and joy of it!

Swimming is not engaged in to enjoy the sensation of floating, or the freshness or coolness of the water. Technique and speed are the goals.

Rather than play active games ourselves, we watch them on television which provides a passive, docile market for the money interests that control sports. Frustration is diverted from channels of social change that deal with the source of frustration into safe release of that energy. Even sports are used to control us.

Marshal McLuhan seems to advocate deeper devotion to electronic fragmentation for those disorganized by technology. But we will not find reality by turning ourselves into an electronic package. Some seem to advocate that you should swallow the dog that bit you. Maybe we need to use our rear-view mirrors and get a new perspective on where we are and where we are going and refuse to be defined by our technological environment.

Technology must be desacralized. Salvation will not

come through reason applied through technology. Uncontrolled technology helped get us into our mess and shows no sign of getting us out. Our attempt to save ourselves at best is like trying to concentrate on falling asleep or trying not to think about something. It is futile. We will not remake ourselves by our own strength or wisdom. That God will do if we would allow it. We will never better ourselves through technology, although neither will we save ourselves by getting rid of it.

We force creation to follow our destiny of slavery and alienation, and attempt to bend nature to our own perverted wills (Romans 8:19-25). We try to control nature and are finding that each action against nature has unknown effects in the environment. In spite of all the advancements in technology and agriculture, there are more poor people on earth than ever before. We have believed that the mastery of technology was a significant way to improve society but forgot the nature of human will and the perverted structures we create in the process.

It is not utopian to think that technology can build new cities with perfect housing, moving streets, an airport on every roof, all physical needs provided through tubes. This is technically possible. But it is utopian to believe that these new cities will be inhabited by better people, that sin and alienation will no longer be part of human existence.

The problems we face are not mere problems, but symptoms of something deeper. Our system (or any system) is not able through technology to solve our problems and provide the good life for us. The talk of many Christians of the need to seek power is sadly an act of conformity to technological values and a faith in the ability of the system to solve our problems.

Technology, like governments, has a tendency toward tyranny. The more technology we develop the more we become dependent upon it, the less independent and free we become, and the more it dominates our lives. It develops a mood of dependency and destroys feelings of creativity. We ignore the extent to which technology determines the shape of social organization and uncritically accept its control. Increasingly it shapes our lives and dictates how we should live.

Consider the tyranny of the clock. The minutest parts of time are measured. It controls our lives, what we do, and when we do it.

Social goals and relationships are subordinated to the techniques we use and determined by them. We even connect our fate to progress. Uncontrolled technology is an enemy of freedom for it results in regimentation and stifles spontaneity. The relationships produced by technology are mechanical rather than organic. Machines give us more outer power but drain our inner energy. We must move beyond technique and qualify it by a set of values and a perspective which does not deny our humanity.

The tyranny also extends to our thought patterns. We have accepted the ultimacy of facts as they are presented to us and seldom dare to question them. They are to be submitted to. Technical experts and science are appealed to as the ultimate justification of what we do.

Technology has perverted science. We have many technicians and few scientists. Science has become the serving maid of the military and economic system. Both social and physical sciences are largely committed to perpetuating what is. Technicans have become the servants of the system and have abdicated almost all morality and responsibility. They only follow orders. They accept the common view that although individuals should not kill, steal, and lie, political and economic institutions may, and so it is acceptable for them to kill, steal, and lie for those institutions.

Modern technology and mechanization have brought alienation. We have destroyed the vital relation between workers and their work. Today most work is neither enjoyable or satisfying. Workers now perform only functional roles which can be changed at any time by someone else.

Technology has taken many skilled workers and reduced them to machine tenders, concerned not about quality but volume. It has virtually destroyed craftsmanship. The industrial revolution transferred production from the workshop and the home into the factory. In the process we destroyed many of the most creative and interesting human skills, destroyed significant institutions, pushed millions into dehumanizing jobs in factories and cut them off from their roots.

Perhaps Gandhi was right in his severe critique of western culture and his conclusion that western-style industrialization must be shunned if India was to gain freedom. He proposed instead development of cottage industries which would avoid the dehumanization of industrialization. He proposed that machines be judged on the basis of their liberating effect on the common people, not on their benefit to those owning the machines.

One can find some hope in Vietnam. The Vietnamese in their determined fight against all the might of American technology have proven that people are still superior to machines. Americans find it difficult to accept that all our force could not subdue the spirit of the Vietnamese people. Maybe that is one reason we bombed, them so intensly. We could not admit that they (especially non-whites) are superior to our machines. Unless our idolatry of technology is humbled there can be no peace in the world.

We must also question the widespread belief that machines and technology reduce work and save time.[2] The amount of work to be done in the world is practically without limit. If a machine does some of our work for us, there is then more work to be done. One

---

[2] I am indebted here to Friedrich Georg Juenger, *The Failure of Technology*, trans. F. D. Wieck (Hinsdale, Ill.: Henry Regnery Co., 1949), pp. 5-8.

then works to maintain the machine, plus do work that otherwise one would never have done. People do more work in an industrial society than in primitive society. The coming of technology and industrialization has actually increased the total work and created employment.

It is true that a machine can produce far more than people working with their hands, but that machine is the end product of a vast amount of work and simply allows more things to be produced. It has not lessened work. Thus far every increase in mechanization has brought an increase in work. People must both create the machines and maintain them. Industrial nations usually are able to pile much of this work on the poor at home and abroad. But machines have not reduced work.

While all this is true, it is not clear that it need be this way. Somehow technology should be able to simplify our lives. But how can we use machines to simplify our lives? We have not yet discovered the way.

We must also question the efficiency of technology. The Amish people reject much of modern technology considered essential to modern farming, yet the Amish are among the most efficient farmers. Modern roads were designed to simplify travel, yet the result has been a new complication of travel. Anyone driving the expressways at rush hour understands that all too well. New techniques carry in themselves demands upon those who use them.

Consider housing. We buy houses that keep us poor and enslaved with payments for years. Renting a house is no cheaper. The American Indians had their wigwams which were warm and comfortable, but they were no burden to them and did not make them poor. We who supposedly are more advanced and better informed (we obviously are not) should be able to devise means of housing which would not be a burden to us. The average person today makes payments for twenty years to buy a house. Is this progress over the wigwam which was constructed in a brief time without debt?

From the perspective of ecology, we are only beginning to realize the havoc that has been created by our technology. The fantastic drain on the world's resources and the rate of pollution cannot be continued. But the vast destruction by technology is nothing compared to the potential destruction through the total mobilization of technology in war. The nightmare of destruction in Vietnam is nothing compared with what we are preparing to do. All told, technology has done little to aid human survival.

The purpose here has not been to completely reject technology, but to call it into question and recognize its limits. Technology is legitimate only as it serves people, as it liberates us for more meaningful relationships. There need be no necessary conflict between the good life and technology. But our acceptance of it should be well planned and with a consciousness of its implications. No machine should ever be accepted uncritically. This means that there will be times when technology will be rejected. We do not need to submit ourselves to the technological-industrial system. We can begin to move to a post-industrial simplicity.

The primary purpose of consumer economic activity is not to provide goods and services, but to keep the system going and produce profit.

Our economy survives only by constantly expanding production and markets. Thus we must consume more and more for the "good of the economy." Whether we need or even desire more consumption is beside the point. We are forced and manipulated to buy more in order to keep the productive process expanding. Consumption and waste are considered a duty. One of the common objections to simplicity is that it would hurt the economy.

But is promoting growth a good thing? Expansion

and growth for its own sake is the pattern of cancer cells. In addition to depleting our resources and polluting our environment, we dehumanize ourselves. Economic life becomes an end in itself rather than a means.

The market psychology dominates all of life. The commodity culture sees everything, including people, as commodities to be bought/sold, manipulated, and thrown away. Even sex is reduced to a means for selling things, an opportunity to exploit another's body, or something to do "just for fun."

When the oppressive nature of consumerism is discussed, some argue that no one is doing it to us; we are only doing it to ourselves. It is true that we have submitted ourselves to the system, but there is more. Consumers have been manipulated by the mass media into craving more and more things they neither need or enjoy. After being told repeatedly that we can never be happy or even human unless we buy Product X, we begin to believe it. False needs and false consciousness are created by something outside ourselves.

Our society takes our deepest feelings and longings (love, sex, acceptance, purpose) and attempts to transform them into commodities to be exploited for profit. This is basic to advertising. We are told we will find love and acceptance if we use the right deodorant. We are told to seek meaning and happiness in those things which have no hope of producing them.

The significant thing about a Barbie Doll is that it is not to be loved and squeezed (it is hard), but primarily suited for wearing clothes. Mattell, Inc., makers of Barbie Dolls, also markets a complete wardrobe for her, thereby teaching little girls the importance of a large variety of fashionable clothes.

Our society awakens hopes in people and then denies their fulfillment. It offers products to fulfill those hopes, but the products can never fill the void. New desires are constantly being created by the process through which they are "fulfilled." People get caught in the cycle of working to buy material things to get ahead to buy more material things. It is not surprising that so many people turn to drugs and violence.

This is not only terribly oppressive for people, but is also a basic contradiction leading to the collapse and overthrow of the present system. One cannot have a healthy society in which the moral integrity of people is undermined by the institutions of that society. Since consumer affluence is unable to satisfy the expectations manufactured by advertising, a deep dissatisfaction emerges that can easily be turned against the system. Dissatisfaction and unfulfilled hopes are the basis for revolution.

The basis of consumerism lies in political powerlessness. Unable to shape our own lives, we are reduced to the function of receptivity. Even our productive ability is turned against us. We are forced to produce and consume in such a way as to guarantee our continued domination. Our productive power is used not for our needs, but for the needs of capitalist expansion. This feeling of powerlessness leads us to compensate by consuming more. People become preoccupied with consuming because this is one seemingly pleasurable activity which is both permitted and encouraged while other more meaningful activity does not seem readily available (actually it is). A poor family might rather have a good house than a new T.V., but since the house is not a possibility, why not enjoy the T.V.?

Consumerism is oppressive not because luxuries are available, but because these luxuries are presented as necessities. It is oppressive because it is more profitable to produce junk to be sold on exploitative installment plans than to produce important products which will improve people's lives. There are reasons why in the "richest" country there are never enough doctors, nurses, or teachers. We are so busy producing, advertising, and consuming the trash we call our standard of living that we do not have the resources for what is important. But we have developed toilet paper that is colored with print design, perfumed and having facial quality.

The consumer economy is a system that in order to survive must create and satisfy false needs at the very time it permits most of the world to live in poverty. The world does not need our consumer aspirations. We must begin attending to the real needs of real people.

The system perpetuates itself through advertising—the engineering of the values, attitudes, and life-styles of our society by a small group of people. Competitive advertising is meant to stimulate buying by creating needs and desires in people that had never before been realized or acted upon. While at one time the purpose of advertising was to inform, now it is to artificially inseminate demand. Thus today most advertising consists of psychological manipulation and outright lies. Little advertising can be considered honest and truthful.

Purchasing commodities has been so sexualized that we are ashamed to carry naked, unwrapped purchases down the street. Why not? Why should we not cover the articles which we were convinced to buy because erotic pleasure was promised to come from them? Is it coincidental that modesty in wrapping has increased while personal modesty with our bodies has decreased?

A big problem facing the advertising and marketing firms is the fact that most of us already have adequate clothes, cars, and refrigerators. The consumer economy cannot wait until these products wear out. Where planned obsolescence has not done the job, psychological obsolescence must be created. Advertisers fight the attitude that a piece of equipment is good as long as it works. We must be made to feel ashamed to drive an old car or wear old clothes. Fashions need to be constantly changed to stimulate sales.

Advertising is a form of domestic imperialism. It both manipulates us into acting against our better interests and makes the products more expensive. In the end, we pay for the advertising. Oppression in refined form remains oppression. People should revolt against this tyranny. We can no longer condone advertisers who play upon anxieties, fears and inferiority feelings to sell their products. The manipulation of human personality means a profound disrespect for persons. A product should be sold simply on its own merits.

Consumerism is an evil system and we need no longer submit to it. It was a course forced upon us by proponents of capitalism and can be reversed. We can make decisions regarding our economic lives. Instead of the slavery of fatalism, we can exercise the freedom to break with set traditions and decide what quality of life we will live.

It is not enough to discuss the consumer economy. We must also discuss its context.

In the United States, consumerism is an expression of corporate capitalism. Since so many people equate capitalism with Christianity (or at least have them married), it is important that we look closer at the values and assumptions of capitalism. It is important also because economic dogmas have replaced religious fanaticism and have become a focus of strife in our world. For many in the west, capitalism has become a religion.

While it is true that the theology of mainline Christianity has given its blessing to capitalism, it is conveniently forgotten that contrary to Max Weber and others, Calvin and the early Calvinists were hostile to the spirit of capitalism. They actually opposed it.[3] It is

---

[3]Albert Hyma, *Christianity, Capitalism and Communism* (Ann Arbor, Mich.: George Wahr, 1937), pp. 135-140. This work also shows the opposition of Luther to much of capitalism and deals extensively with the church's view of economics throughout history. For a historical discussion of Christianity and economics also see Guy Franklin Hershberger, *The Way of the Cross in Human Relations* (Scottdale, Pa.: Herald Press, 1958).

usually ignored that Calvin placed severe limitations on economic activity. He condemned concentrations of wealth and luxury and was severe in his denunciation of the merchant princes. The Anabaptists and other Christian radicals also opposed capitalism. Medieval Catholicism even opposed the charging of interest, a practice condemned by the Bible.

One cannot identify Christianity with capitalism, but neither can it be identified with any other economic form, including socialism. All economic systems must come under the judgment of God. No particular economic system can be equated with the kingdom of God and be baptized, but some are clearly in direct opposition to the Christian vision. This is especially true of capitalism.

The capitalism we are here analyzing is not the robber baron capitalism of John D. Rockefeller. Actually even he opposed individualism and free enterprise and pushed for a centralized, collective economy. Laissez-faire capitalism is past even though its ideology remains. We live not in a "free economy," but in a collectivized, planned economy controlled by private power. We are describing modern corporate capitalism which consists of socialism for the rich and free enterprise for the poor. We are analyzing the structure of the consumer society.

How does capitalism conflict with Christian theology?

In our society, capitalism is a system that competes with God for our loyalty. Capitalism is a materialistic philosophy and system that is in rebellion against God and is based on no moral commitment except materialistic success.

Capitalism is based on unchristian theological assumptions. It assumes that people (some people) are basically good and rational and can progressively shape nature and history to their own will. In essence, this is an atheistic understanding of history with progress seen as inevitable as long as economic laws are allowed to function uninhibited. It clearly sees people, not God, in control of history. Through uninhibited economic striving people can work out their own salvation. Adam Smith wrote that society can be best organized if each person "intends only his own gain," if each person looks after one's own interests.

If people were not sinners this might not be totally unrealistic, but it would still be unchristian. The Apostle Paul wrote, "Let no one seek his own good, but the good of his neighbor" (1 Corinthians 10:24). The Christian cannot accept self-interest as a moral basis for economic activity or any other kind of ethical choices. The truth is that people are sinners and their selfish interests need to be disciplined. The history of capitalism and its step-child, imperialism, have demonstrated that too well.

God never intended people to live a self-centered life. While personal gain is the motivation of the old age, those who live in the new age are called to something better. The Christian is called to a life of love, sharing, and service to others. Christians will also reject the individualistic spirit of capitalism. Rather than putting the individual first, the Christian puts God first. Rather than living for oneself, we are called to community, to a life of common sharing. The basic theology of capitalism is unchristian.

At the heart of capitalism is the profit motive. Profit has been substituted for service as the key to relationships with others. This has meant the undermining of Christian values. The good becomes equated with what is profitable. We decide what is to be done or not done on the basis of what is most profitable, not by what best serves human needs. We have pollution partly because corporations find it more profitable to pollute than to take necessary steps to stop it. Only those things that can be measured in financial terms are given priority.

With the coming of capitalism much that had formerly been considered sin—greed, avarice, gluttony, envy and jealousy—came to be considered cardinal virtues because they were incentives to industrial growth. Thus capitalism stimulates and encourages the lower elements in human nature. The spirit of selfishness is rewarded.

The profit motive has perverted many areas of our lives. Consider technology. Most machines that could be used to improve life are used for the profit of a few, not the many. Consider the auto industry's refusal up to this point to build pollution-free cars or the subverting of mass transit by many powerful corporations. The reason we do not have inexpensive housing for the poor is that it is not profitable for the rich. Machines could be made more simple, but they are made increasingly complex so that ordinary people cannot fix them. Many professions (*e.g.*, medical and building trades), in order to maintain a high salary, work actively to prevent more people from becoming trained and try to keep their expertise away from the common people in order to be "worth more money."

Capitalism encourages competition. It rewards those who are aggressive and penalizes those who value cooperation. Thus conflict and combat are encouraged and glorified. Competition creates conflicts of interests, markets and resources, and reaches its climax in war.

Rather than the survival of the fittest, the Bible points to caring for the unfit. Even Darwin understood that mutual aid and cooperation are important, both for animals and humans, for the survival of the species. In the sinking of the Titanic, woman and children were to be saved first. This is an expression of cooperation and the desire to preserve the species. Times of great difficulty and distress often bring forth a new sense of community. The need to cooperate to survive becomes apparent.

Competition is antisocial. When one has experienced group process without the competitive spirit, the antisocial nature of competition is apparent. In intellectual pursuits the best results are attained by cooperation. Science is built on this. When children grab things from each other and declare, "This is mine," parents try to teach them to share. When these children grow up and grab for themselves, we praise them for being industrious. Christian faith stresses sharing and cooperation, not competition.

Capitalism means exploitation. Competition is the struggle to dominate and oppress with the resulting dynamic of domination/submission. It perpetuates the roles of boss/worker, strong/weak, rich/poor. Capitalist governments give special privileges to the powerful to aid them in their struggle to gain more power, thus guaranteeing inequities and making it impossible for many to rise above a subsistence level. Competition among unequals develops domination of the strong and subservience among the weak.

Capitalism is individual selfishness organized into class selfishness. Consider the results. Internationally it has meant imperialism (the reason for United States military presence around the world) and exploitation of the Third World. Domestically it has meant perpetuation of poverty and the subjugation of all classes to a one-dimensional perspective, an affliction imposed on both ghetto and suburb. The results have been disastrous.

Militarism and racism are only two examples. Consider how people turn on each other, how one group is pitted against another, how fear and distrust are encouraged. These are not accidents. They are a logical outgrowth of the structural relationships produced by our society. With the encouragement of competition, and yet being dominated in the process, the aggressiveness of capitalist people is directed against any possible target, be it Jew or foreigner, black or communist, and especially anyone who presents an alternative to the system they are so bound to. To a large extent the high crime rates in poor areas are expressions of misplaced hostility toward the powerful in society but directed toward one's own group instead. Not only has capitalism meant the exploitation of the poor; it has dehumanized and exploited every class.

Equality is incompatible with capitalism. In the competitive struggle some are bound to end up on the bottom. Capitalism would not exist if there were equality. The result is fantastic wealth for some and deprivation for others. Any system that not only permits but also encourages the vast separation of rich and poor must be rejected.

Capitalism forces some to struggle for survival and encourages laziness in others. While some starve, others receive huge amounts of money without working. The government gives massive assistance to the rich. For the rich it is called subsidies while a small amount for the poor is called welfare. One man in California has been receiving four million dollars a year in farm subsidies. Others get it through speculation, playing the stock market, or from interest on money they never worked to earn. These people, not the poor, are parasites on society, living on the hard work of others. A Christian cannot accept the inequality that goes with capitalism.

Capitalism means not only the alienation of rich and poor, but also the alienation of work. The working class may have been given consumer affluence, but their oppression continues. It has transformed an economy of independent workers into a mass of hired employees who are forced to sell their labor to employers upon whom they are dependent for survival. They work not for themselves but for the boss they resent.

Human labor, which should be creative and a means of self-expression, has been transformed into a system of repetitive, mindless activity. People are forced to work in unnecessary and dehumanizing jobs. While there is much meaningful work to be done, most are forced into vapid jobs, doing work that is either useless or harmful to others. This includes many white collar jobs. People have been subordinated to economic priorities and as such are considered useful or useless (justification by work and production instead of grace). Creative initiative has been suppressed in all but a few.

Freedom is defined as the ability to participate in one's own exploitation, to accept the controls of the system. In spite of all the consumer affluence workers may be "rewarded" with, they do not own or have any control over what they produce. Workers are alienated from each other in the process of competing with each other. Capitalism programs people into a managed, closed society which denies them any significant voice in what their future will be or participation in creating it. It uses people for its own purposes rather than helping people serve each other and God.

In its emphasis on private property, capitalism denies that all physical resources belong to God and we are only to be stewards of them. It encourages us to say, "This is mine, I will do with it what I wish." The story of two capitalists on a boat in the middle of the ocean makes the point well. One came to the other and said, "You know the boat is sinking?" The other replied, "Don't worry, it doesn't belong to us."

The Christian view of property is stewardship, with responsibility to God and our brothers and sisters. Actually, capitalism is not consistent in its value of private property. If private property is so important, why not see that everyone has a fair portion of it instead of hoarding all we can for ourselves?

Capitalism is undemocratic. Under capitalism, power comes from possession. The result has been the creation of huge concentrations of power that are not responsible to anyone but themselves. Corporations have tremendous amounts of power but are not responsible to the people they affect. Most businesses and factories are run as dictatorships rather than as democracies. Capitalism assumes that society should be controlled by an impersonal market rather than be directed by people cooperating with each other. De Tocqueville was right when he said, "Preoccupation with material things is the mother of tyranny."

Capitalism is wasteful. It is wasteful in its rape of nature, production of junk for profit, planned obsolescence, and competition. We do not need twenty brands of shaving cream. Under the current system it is cheaper for individual corporations to produce new materials than recycle. But the cost to the environment and to society is enormous and we do pay for it. When profit is more important than stewardship, waste is inevitable.

It is important that we move beyond capitalism. The means of production and distribution must be subordinated to the requirements of human solidarity and community. Production should be for meeting social needs, not accumulation of wealth. No longer should the desire for profit be a basis for economic activity. Cooperation and community must be valued above competition and coercion. Economic structures need to be democraticized and wealth distributed.

People can begin to share with each other rather than living for themselves. It is significant that the most beautiful acts of service and sharing and the most unpleasant tasks usually carry with them little or no monetary remuneration. Where would the world be without unselfish deeds, without those who are never paid for their service? May such foolishness increase!

Just as chattel slavery was abandoned as an economic base and monarchy as a form of government, so our present economic system must give way to something new. And it is. Capitalist culture is already collapsing. Next will come the breakdown of the economic and political structures that still stand. The sensate culture is dying while a new society is being born in its midst.

CHAPTER 6

Life-styles and Revolution

WE LIVE IN APOCALYPTIC TIMES AND LIKE
similar times in the past, many groups are breaking
from the dominant culture and experimenting with new
life-styles. As a new consciousness begins to emerge,
people begin to see the contradictions between the new
and the old. As the old structures and values lose their
legitimacy the new is seen as possible.

This phenomenon is very much in evidence today
and takes many forms. Some see the need for a political revolution in which the control of the power structures is taken over by the oppressed so that a new society can be created. Others see political concerns to
be a distraction or even the enemy of building a new
society. Thus the changing of one's life-style can be considered to be the revolution, to be irrelevant, or even
to be the enemy of the revolution. We now examine
these options more closely and then show how simplicity can relate to revolution. The point of view developed here sees the need for change to be both cultural
and political.

First we look at the importance of the political.

An a-political stance leads to an a-moral stance. We
have seen that demonstrated all too well in the
watered-down, feeble religion that goes by the name
of Christianity in all too many churches. Whether it is
conservative culture religion or youth culture, if it becomes a-political or a-historical, the struggle for liberation is soon lost. It is important to remember that the

134

Biblical view sees salvation as historical and that God is at work in the events of history.

An a-political position cannot lead to liberation, for it ignores a large part of our being. Social structures do help determine the nature and quality of relationships and force good people into oppressive relationships. True liberation relates to all of life. Thus to be serious about liberation is to change our relationship also to the social structures. When a world view or religion becomes individualistic and purely personal, people easily submit to the collective and structural aspects of oppression. The counter culture cannot ignore politics. It will be involved in resistance or conform. The revolution will not be won without discipline and struggle. The political aspect is essential.

But the concept of political revolution is also filled with dangers.

Too often we see the problem *out there* and forget that we are the problem, that we must change.

We should never forget that the revolution we seek is not to substitute one authoritarian structure and world view for another. There is little point in reproducing the hierarchies of the old order and submitting ourselves to leadership styles that reflect the relations of capitalism. Rather we need to learn to break submissive patterns of behavior. Most all the political revolutions to date have not liberated people. No group has seized power and then voluntarily given it back to the people. Those who seek to achieve their goal through political power find themselves surrendering more and more to the state and end up with little freedom. Centralized political power is the opposite of freedom. To a large extent the political revolutionaries want a revolution which will be a climax to the processes of our historical development rather than one which will reverse the course of history. A true revolution rejects the direction of our whole society and develops new patterns.

Those who try to destroy the present system are taking it too seriously and investing too much energy on it. Our commitment is not to the destruction of the old system, but by acting as the midwife in the birth of the new. One replaces the old system not by imitating it, but by building upon a new vision.

Resistance is important. There is no liberation without it. But resistance is not liberation. It is merely saying no. The liberated person can also say yes. Resistance is confession. It is clearing away the entanglements that prevent a liberated life-style. It is clearing the way. It is not *the* way.

Since the problem of our society is more than political, the solution must also be more than political.

A revolution is nothing if it is not cultural. If the structures are changed, but not the values and relationships, the same type of oppressive structures will emerge. Revolution must be a total organic process through which a new society comes into being. A complete transformation of culture is also called for.

Capitalism is more than an organization of bankers and industrialists. It involves values, attitudes, and patterns of action. It is a way of life. Every one of us has to a large extent internalized those structures, presuppositions, and values. Thus we need to rid ourselves of those values and loyalties and make a real change in our life-styles. Liberation is constantly both an external and internal struggle. But it is always our struggle. Rather than aiding others paternalistically in their struggle, we need to see the struggle in terms of our own liberation and survival and then see how that is related to others in their struggle.

Oppression is more than material. People are not only controlled in the factory, but cultural forms have been established to maintain submission to oppression. It is revolutionary to reject those cultural forms and to develop liberating ones.

A change of heart is needed. But if a change of heart has taken place it will be evidenced in outward relationships and action. If the change has taken place in the heart, then the commitment to old values and structures will not remain intact. Liberation means that we become new people, recognizing that what we have been was destructive both to ourselves and to others. This means finding new identities, new values, new goals. With a new self-identity we will not readily buy into the old.

Revolutionizing human relationships, values, and life-styles simply cannot wait for a political revolution. Indeed, our humanity is one of the essential ingredients in making political changes. We need not wait until after some great apocalyptic event to begin changing our lives. Rather than only analyzing revolution, we can be living it.

We must struggle simultaneously against the enslavement of a materialistic society as well as against the alienated and distorted relationships between persons. Unless we can make it a human struggle, it is almost inevitable that we will be absorbed by the values of the old system. The problem with most groups is that they cannot find a combination of political action and a loving community that is able to deal with personal needs. Could it be that this is the reason so many groups fall apart? Either they lose contact with each other or lose contact with history.

We must also take a critical look at the cultural revolution for it is quite questionable whether the current youth culture will lead to meaningful social change.

The question is not whether cultural revolution is necessary, but what form it will take. The real question is whether the culture revolution is a superficial change in life-style or whether it goes to the very root and foundations of society.

It appears to be superficial. There is nothing revolutionary in paying fifteen dollars for a rock concert. That is bourgeois privilege. Freedom is not just in growing long hair and a beard, in not wearing a bra, or even in rejecting middle-class values. Much more is needed than the trinkets of youth culture.

Much of the counter culture is a mirror of the worst features of the old sick society. The revolution is not free dope, free sex, and abortions on demand. That is the dying gasps of an old culture and will not lead to new life. The pseudo-libertarian eroticism, elements of sado-masochism, and sexist advertisements in much of the underground press is part of the perversion of the old order and an expression of death. Many in the underground are living the same values of the establishment, only in inverted form. Drugs and electronic music are not a revolutionary response to a society that finds its basic meaning in consumption!

Life-style revolution carries the danger of ignoring the reality of the system and failing to come to grips with it. It too much accepts a separation between personal and social dimensions of life. There is always the danger of thinking of ourselves as liberated rather than in the process of being liberated. It is easier to enjoy music with others than to struggle with them. In the search for the good life one cannot ignore the reality of evil and suffering. The counter culture is profound in its refusal of the old. Whether it refuses enough and what it accepts must also be questioned.

Life-styles are easy to co-opt. Note how many are becoming rich from the symbols of the youth culture and how those symbols have become marketable. Rock music has produced a new generation of capitalists. The system is hiring people from the counter culture to help them understand youth so that they can adjust their image to appeal to the youth. That is not revolution.

It should not be forgotten that the system will try either to absorb or exterminate all anomalies rather than permit basic change. The easiest method is to change the form without changing the substance. Note all the ecology ads by the greatest polluters. Cultural fads can easily be used as a new method of integrating rebellious youth into the system. The system will use even the symbols of rebellion to depoliticize us. The same tactic is used against those working for political change. The system can even adapt itself to the concept of worker power in the form of conservative labor unions.

We must ask those involved in change of life-style whether this is only an escape, a safety valve. To what extent do their actions challenge the basis and presuppositions of the whole system? Does it produce forces that cannot be ignored by the larger society? How easily can it be bought off? Does it create an illusion of freedom and permissiveness within the system? How does it change the consciousness of the participants?

One current middle-class expression of the life-style thrust is sensitivity groups. While they are obviously a response to a real need, it is questionable whether they point toward much meaningful change. Sensitivity is an important value, but as with most everything else in a technological society, a good thing has been transformed into a technique. We simulate close relationships and play being close instead of experiencing authentic relationships. Openness and depth sharing are too serious to be played with in a weekend encounter group composed of people whom you have never seen before and will never see again. The word that best describes paying for depth sharing with strangers without any commitment is "prostitution." Warm feelings of acceptance become a substitute for the real thing in community.

Deep sharing takes on authenticity only in the context of a group of people who are committed to each other. Sensitivity groups are an a-political method of dealing with human problems and are often an escape from reality. Alienation will not be overcome simply by strangers either emotionally or physically fondling each other. Authoritarianism and repression will not be overcome with friendliness in the context of institutionalized permissiveness without confronting the outside world. Usually this means a denial of the depth of alienation and repression that exists.

Being a-political, sensitivity groups are unconcerned with historical perspectives. They, like fundamentalist religion, are concerned primarily with personal salvation. The important questions concerning our commitments and loyalties are not raised. Like other cultural forms, sensitivity training is highly marketable, but of little political significance, except as an escape valve to help people cope with (rather than reject) the oppressiveness of our society. Actually these groups are often very authoritarian and encourage conformist tendencies.

Yet we dare not completely reject the pietistic approach of small groups searching for vitality within the existing structures. Such movements do create new possibilities for breaking with the system and can produce radical shifts within the culture. Consider the pietist reaction to Lutheran scholasticism or the romantic reaction to rationalism. Pietism can be revolutionary if it leads to transformation of persons, creation of new values and institutions, and the transfer of authority from the system to a new community. It is not irrelevant to save individuals out of a society that is disintegrating.

The revolution we seek must be related to all of life. It is all-encompassing in its call for change and transformation. It can leave no area of our sickness unhealed.

A political revolution is nothing if it does not bring fundamental changes in the culture and a cultural revolution is meaningless if it brings no change in the political structures. The whole framework of society needs to be changed, including attitudes and values.

We must reject both the way of political power struggles and an a-political stance. A life-style revolution that ignores political-structural questions will be shallow and usually lead away from involvement and action towards retreat and accommodation. Also, the road of spiritualism and mysticism does not lead to liberation.

While the culture people run the danger of being bought off by the system, the politicals run the danger of violence and manipulation, of becoming like the system in its hardened values. To get completely caught up in the structural and forget the wider aspects of life is to be narrow and to lead to inhuman activities. The structures will never be liberated unless we are liberated.

A balance is needed between the personal and the collective, between the rational and nonrational. The cure for sickly inwardness is social responsibility while the cure for frantic outwardness is a new discovery of the inward.

The revolution must begin with us.

We need to incorporate within our own lives the revolution we seek. We need not only a theory of a liberated society, but the practice of it. We need the experience of living a new reality. Instead of talking about abstract ideals, we can begin to live a new life. The time has come for a change and it must begin with me.

Revolutionary groups not only talk of the future, but begin to live that future. They demonstrate that what is coming is more genuine and real than the present order which is passing away. They live on the boundary of the collapse of the old and the emergence of the new. There the new humanity and the new society is already beginning to emerge. The Word is in the process of becoming flesh. Jesus Christ is laying the foundation of the new humanity that He will bring into being.

The society we envision is already reflected in the nature of the struggle that has begun. Our actions point to the kind of society we hope for. Our means are in harmony with the end we see coming. Our efforts for peace and justice will do little good if done in the spirit of the old order. In that case our efforts will only help continue the destruction, not end it.

As we become liberated from the old consciousness new self identities emerge. We act out of a new consciousness which liberates us from the old mindset. We are then free for new possibilities. And as we act out of that new consciousness, the possibility of a new consciousness in the larger society becomes an option.

It is important that we begin to create new forms and institutions that will incorporate the new consciousness and new values. Unless these become concrete, they will have little meaning and will soon be absorbed by the dominant culture. When we concretely begin to change our lives and allow our vision to be expressed in alternate forms, there is less chance that we will be bought off by society: It is much more difficult to co-opt disfunctional structures than abstract ideas. It is imperative that we begin to create liberated zones where we can live out our lives in the context of space, resources, and time that have been liberated. We can begin to do already what is yet unthinkable for the rest of society.

There is no one correct thing to be doing. Rather, thousands of people and groups should be doing thousands of different things which they see contributing to the creation of new alternatives. In the end, genuine actions do converge. History is not produced so much by great dramatic events as by patient work over a long period of time. What takes the longest time may be the most significant. True, the changes are infinitesimal in comparison with the change needed in the total society. But even one example is significant and we can never know what effect it will have. If we see our actions as an organic part of a larger movement Christ is leading, we can proceed with hope.

What is needed now is experimentation with new forms. The current experiments with free schools, food co-ops, cottage industries, communes, and radical church communities all point in the right direction. Many of them may fail, but we can learn from the failures. Start to experiment in those areas that concern and interest you most.

It is important that the new alternatives we create be related to the old. Unless new communities are in tension with the old they will likely soon become ingrown and separated from history. It is important that the new express a basic contradiction to the larger society and be disfunctional for it. The very existence of the new should point to the transformation of the old.

Remember that the signs of the new always threaten the existing order. Where you find the greatest good, there the forces of evil concentrate themselves and are at work. New structures which are incompatible with the surrounding oppressive society are never immune from attacks. Preparation should be made to deal with attempts to crush or repress movements for social change. That means that we build relationships and structures in such a way that, short of killing all the people involved, the system is completely powerless to destroy the new alternatives. We need to develop new structures that will be more powerful than the present establishment. But for this to happen it cannot be done on the terms of the old order. Using the methods of the system we do not have a chance.

Our approach does not include coercion. That is part of the old order we reject. Coercion does not lead to new life and transformation, but rather perpetuates submissiveness and hardens opposition. The new life we seek must be voluntary. Only a voluntary society can be a free society.

There are two kinds of power. One is the means to force people to act contrary to their wishes. This power is a rope, a chain, a whip. It is intimidation, coercion, extortion and direct violence. It is political power as we know it today. The second kind of power is the courage for people to act according to their best vision regardless of institutions. This is the best meaning of "power to the people." Evil can be subdued only by love and goodness. The sword is not an acceptable method for social change. The cross is more to the point.

Our strategy for social change is to reject the old, begin to live in the new, create new alternatives within a committed community, and then to live in tension and confrontation with the old. This is nothing new. There have been many examples in history of groups which abandoned the structures of the status quo and created new alternatives. Consider Moses, Jesus and the early church, the Anabaptists, and the Quakers.

We will never get very far if we cannot present a living alternative to unsatisfying jobs, suffocating education, and strangling consumerism. Few people will act on the basis of a call to self-sacrifice. But people can be called to join a community which provides the opportunities for sharing, loving, and living in a way never before thought quite possible. When we catch that vision, we can begin to live it with our brothers and sisters. By God's grace we can live the good life now and seek first His kingdom.

CHAPTER 7

Putting First Things First

CHRISTIAN FAITH AFFIRMS THAT THE GOOD LIFE cannot be found by striving for it. Hedonism (be it enlightened or the more degenerate varieties) is a dead-end street. Rather the good life comes to us as a gift, a by-product of leaving the old behind to follow a new vision. Jesus put it well when he told people, "Seek first his kingdom . . . and all these things shall be yours as well" (Matthew 6:33).

To seek first the kingdom is to have a singleness of purpose rather than trying to go in twelve directions at once. Simple means single. Divided loyalties destroy simplicity. In the story of the man from whom Jesus cast the demons in Mark 5, the demoniac said his name was Legion, because he was many. He was torn in many directions.

Kierkegaard said that purity of heart is to will one thing. To will one thing is to will the good, for only good has unity. Evil is disunity. It leads to chaos. To desire any evil thing is not to will one thing, for it divides us. To do what is not good does not satisfy and so leads to many other things. Simplicity implies pure motives.

Singleness can only be found in relation to God, for he is the source of unity and the essence of simplicity. To will one thing will mean unconditional loyalty to God. His creation was unified, the expression of simplicity. The Jerusalem Bible translates Ecclesiastes 7:29 as ". . . God made man simple; man's complex problems are of his own devising." Humanity brought division into the world because of its rebellion against God. Adam and Eve lived a simple life until they broke their unity with God. Then they lost their simplicity.

To seek first the kingdom gives us the clarity of sight to distinguish between the important and unimportant, the primary and secondary, the essential and superfluous. It is to grasp what is essential and to see ourselves in relation to that. This insight makes irrelevant much of what complicates our lives.

To seek first the kingdom gives a centeredness to our lives. There is something that holds things together, a unifying perspective. To simplify is to focus. We have two eyes, but if they function properly, there is a unity of vision. To see double is disunity and the loss of simplicity. Focusing does not narrow one's vision, nor reduce our energies, but brings unity to them by concentrating them.

To seek first the kingdom means our lives will have a direction. We will begin to see the purpose of our lives pointing to the east or west, to the left or right. But if we are to travel westward, we must leave behind many good things in the east. If we are serious about a new life it is imperative that we cut ourselves off from all that would hold us back. We need to have a dream and follow it.

To seek first the kingdom is to live free from all entanglements that prevent us from responding to the Light. Faithfulness to God, to one's vision, comes before all other loyalties. Thus the religious person will discard everything that stands in the way of faithfulness. Nothing may come between us and God.

This is exactly what is meant by giving up worship of false gods. We will not allow our commitment to be distorted or faded by any distraction. We will have the freedom to practice holy obedience and not be encumbered or diverted by other commitments. We will allow our spiritual life to condition our economic life rather than letting our spiritual life be conditioned by the economic.

The simple life is an uncluttered life. Clutter is anything that keeps me from doing what I am called to do, anything that destroys harmony within me, with my brothers and sisters or with God. It is those things which take away my freedom and enslave me. The simple life then is the result of clearing away all the rubble which prevents my growing in new life.

This requires a deep commitment to God. Only those who are committed will not be tossed about by the pressures of our society. The simple person acts in relation to a commitment and sense of purpose. Simplicity is perseverance (stick-to-it-iveness) and persistence. One does not keep jumping from one thing to another, but keeps pushing toward a goal. Simplicity is to take the leap of faith. It is to commit oneself.

To seek first the kingdom, to be committed, is more than the result of our own efforts.

We can deny all material possessions, live in austere simplicity and share everything with the poor, but if this is not an authentic expression of a transformed life, it is empty.

Our very being has been shaped by the consumer society and so the problem is not only our complex environment, but also our own entangled lives. Escape to a quiet South Sea island would be of little help to us. We would carry our complexities and fever with us. Our lives need to be changed. We need liberation from the slavery into which we have been trapped.

Simplicity is the outgrowth of a profound reality in our lives that radically changes our relation to the world around us. When we are grasped by a new meaning of life, the old superficial things begin to fall away. When we walk in the Light, the frivolous and unnecessary lose their grip on us. The unreal no longer has any attraction for us. The more we have to live for, the less we need to live on.

Simplicity is primarily a state of being, not only something we do. The source is internal, not external.

We can adopt all the outward forms (riding a bicycle, growing our own food) and never get to the real life. In such a case we find ourselves acting a role instead of living authentically. If our life-styles are not based on a conversion of the heart, they are bound to be not only sterile, but legalistic and self-righteous. We are called primarily not to act, but to be. Never action for action's sake or simplicity for simplicity's sake, but action that comes out of our being. Buddha's statement, "Don't just do something, stand there," is most appropriate. Simplicity is a state of consciousness and awareness. If we have not found simplicity in our inner being, we will not find it in our daily lives.

That new reality is not something we create. We do not re-create (save) ourselves by our good works, including simplicity. Then the result could be pride, self-righteousness, and smugness. Our use or non-use of things will not liberate us. Simplicity is the result of the releasing power of a new reality.

We must get to the source of life in order to be set free. All that we do must be an expression of our encounter with the Light. That Source of life, that Light, is Jesus Christ. It is in personal encounter with Him that our lives are transformed. Only through Him can we be liberated from all slavery and have our desires reversed. When God becomes a reality in our lives, the clutter falls away. Only as we are connected to the Source of life do we get a true perspective on what life is. Only as we are liberated from anxiety and worry by a faith in God can we overcome the tyranny of greed.

We will never find fullness of life by following our twisted desires. Our natural will needs to be subjected to the divine in order to be made whole. Our own will needs to be bent to that Will which is greater than ours. Many object to this and do not want their wills bent in any way. They see this as a violation of the self. But this position can be maintained only if one can say that one's will is truly straight and does not need bending to make it straight. God can bend our wills without violating us. We can be reborn and our new wills are still truly our own. Only in Christ can we find our true selves.

That new birth is not the shallow emotional experience talked about by many popular preachers who do not seem to understand how one's life can be transformed or what the new age is all about. Those who bless killing peasants in Southeast Asia obviously have missed the depth of what transformation and the new birth is all about. If the heart is changed, it will show in all one's relationships. The radical transformation that comes from encounter with the living Christ changes one's whole life. That includes the economic and political. We should be careful not to spiritualize the new birth and say that the only important thing is that your heart is right. If our heart is right our outer condition will be radically changed.

It is important that we do not reject the consumer society out of a nostalgic longing for a primitive existence or a romantic idea of the happy savage. Simplicity is not a return to nature, but a return to God. There is a difference. The more one moves away from God and an understanding of transcendence, the more one moves toward a one-dimensional view of reality. It is in relation to God that our perspectives are deepened and broadened.

The kingdom of God is available as a gift to us. There is no complicated way to achieve it. It is just as available to the poor as to the rich (actually more so). In fact, the only way to receive the gift of new life is through simply accepting it. The question is whether we are willing to receive the new life that is available to us.

Seeking first the kingdom is not asceticism.

Christian simplicity is no more ascetic than an athlete preparing for a race. The athlete takes off all non-essential clothing, is careful about eating and concentrates on what is important in reaching the prize. Those called to run a race must lay aside every weight. That is not asceticism.

The issue is not self-sacrifice or deprivation. Unless you give up things out of a sense of freedom, you will probably continually want them back. Even after you have given them up, you are not free from them, for they still have power over you. Although it cannot be documented, William Penn is supposed to have asked George Fox if it were right for him to continue to wear his ceremonial sword (a sign of nobility). George is said to have answered, "Wear it as long as thee can." George expected him to give it up and he did.

If you are convinced that something (*e.g.*, books) is helping, not hindering, you to live the good life then keep them as long as you can. But do not rationalize! And do give them up when they are no longer helpful. Be willing to give them up now; otherwise they have power over you.

To let go of the old life will not always be easy. At times we need to give up things even if it is hard. Sometimes we have created blocks to grace and need to take a first step so that new life can be given to us. Sometimes we need to will something before we desire it. Maybe we will understand how enslaved we have been only after we have let go.

Although we are not basing simplicity on any concept of sacrifice, we are not denying the validity of sacrifice. At times sacrifice is called for. Something must be said in recognition of those people who are sealing their commitment with great personal sacrifice and suffering. Those who are in prison, exile, or underground give all of us much to ponder in the way they have burned behind them many bridges to security. When involved in a struggle for liberation, sacrifice is necessary.

We will at times give up our desires so that we will not further contribute to and support the oppression of others. Not eating grapes during the grape boycott, even though one craves grapes, is a good example. Even sacrifice can be joyful. On the other hand, we must not make sacrifice an absolute value and thus feel guilty when we are not suffering.

Nor is this to say that pleasure is to be equated with good and suffering with evil. We do not desire suffering, but realize that it is not most to be feared. Submission to slavery and oppression are much worse. It is worse to be unfaithful than to suffer. Often suffering can lead to victory. Every denial of self is not asceticism.

There are many things that we will give up. There will be no money for night clubs, cocktail parties, new Cadillacs, and mink coats. It will mean giving up status striving and social competition. But so what? We give up all not in a mood of sacrifice, but with the promise that new life will be given to us. If we give up our false securities, more profound securities will be given to us. If, instead of hedonistically seeking happiness, we seek God, we will find happiness.

A note of caution must be raised, however. When we give up status, draft cards, or comfortable conditions, it is important that we do it not out of a mere sense of duty or with a feeling of superiority over others, but in a spirit of celebration. If we go to prison, let us go joyfully. If we give up our draft cards, let it be a liberating experience, not a burden. Give up what you have, not to get rid of guilt, but to free yourself to live a new life. Give up things because they are preventing you from being faithful. Whatever you do, do it with joy in your heart.

We do what we cannot keep from doing. True martyrs do not seek martyrdom and suffering. It comes to them uninvited as a consequence of their liberated life. Simplicity is not a suppression of our deepest longings, but the fulfillment of them. The good life is the simplicity of fulfillment, not impoverishment.

Seeking first the kingdom leads to the good life.

Those who are humble and live simply are more likely to find peace, satisfaction, and meaning than those who aspire to fame and wealth. It is not a coincidence that many of the wisest and most imaginative people throughout history have lived the simplest lives. In contrast to the monotonous existence of most people, those who live simply find life challenging and fulfilling. The more things we can do without, the richer we can become.

Joy and happiness are not in things, but in us and in other people. Wealth and richness is a state of being rather than possession. Riches are what I am and what I can become. If they are what I have, they can be taken away. If they are what I am, they can never be taken from me.

The standard of living should be thought of in terms of quality of life—what brings happiness, growth, maturity—rather than quantity of things. We need not more, but less and better. The good life is an unencumbered, uncluttered, disentangled life. The good life cannot be bought with money. This means that much in our society is a fraud. The prophet Isaiah put it well:

> Ho, every one who thirsts,
>   come to the waters;
> and he who has no money,
>   come, buy and eat!
> Come, buy wine and milk
>   without money and without price.
> Why do you spend your money for
>   that which is not bread,
> and your labor for that
>   which does not satisfy?
>   *Isaiah 55:1-2*

Simplicity is found to the extent we live life fully. The empty life is not simple. But as our lives are filled with meaning and purpose, the void and complexity is overcome.

Think of the simplicity that comes with love. While love is not easy and carries with it responsibility, love does simplify life and bring unity. Hate complicates life and brings disunity.

Simplicity includes contentment and patience. It is the calmness of the sick and handicapped who have come to terms with their problems. Simplicity is the ability to wait. Confucius said,

> Here is a man whose desires are few. In some things he will not be able to maintain his resolution, but they will be few. Here is a man whose desires arc many. In some things he will be able to maintain his resolution, but they will be few.[1]

This is not the contentment of a lizard sleeping in the sun. Nor is it a rationale for submitting to oppression. It is the patience to endure a long struggle. Even the rebel can already find peace, joy, and liberation.

Simplicity implies order. Not the complicated and regimented order of "law and order" which merely encircles chaos, but the deep order that freely evolves out of truth and authentic relationships. Violence oversimplifies, but never makes things more simple. The result is that violence complicates. Simplicity is an answer to chaos based on fear, disunity, and hate.

With a little more use of our intelligence, much more wisdom, and a complete change of heart, we could take the materials of our civilization and provide for everyone's material *needs* comfortably without the slavery and degradation of compulsive consumption. We could transform some of the products of our civili-

---

[1]Quoted by Richard B. Gregg, *The Value of Voluntary Simplicity* (Wallingford, Pa.: Pendle Hall Pamphlets, 1936), p. 26.

zation into a blessing rather than the curse they are today.

If we seek first the kingdom, we will find liberation and freedom.

The simple life is an expression of liberation from the domination of the profit-seekers over our lives. It is freedom from the tyrannical assumptions of affluent society. The good news is that we can be liberated from all that binds us and oppresses us.

Bourgeois living is only for the slaves who are not allowed to travel. The free people are on a pilgrimage. But to be a pilgrim, one cannot take along any excess baggage. When you add the unnecessary, you are no longer a pilgrim. You have become a slave. Eberhard Arnold had this vision when he wrote,

> I know a land, not far away
>   midst country bare and cold,
> The wilderness hems in its hills
>   where seekers dig for gold.
> Earth's richest treasure comes to men
>   with courage to unite,
> Gold-veins of depths we never dreamed
>   yield riches pure and bright.
>
> The road to this new land
>   is only free for him to find
> Who travels free from all his goods,
>   who left them all behind.
> The goods he owned in his old land,
>   he gave to those in need,
> His will broke loose from selfish bonds—
>   for Christ, who died and freed.
>
> His kingdom beckons us to come
>   and share its childlike joys,
> Joy shatters soon the time-worn ways,
>   and "yours" and "mine" destroys.

He is the greatest fool on earth
who to his riches clings,
He gropes in blindness, black as night—
and death of heart it brings.[2]

What a joy it is to be free from concern about
things, status, and fashions. They are hard masters
waiting for us to become their slaves. To the extent we
become dependent on them, we are enslaved by them.
People become slaves of jobs, possessions, monthly
payments. Freedom is much more than the right to
own and dispose of material things at will.

There is no slavery as tyrannical as personal desires.
We are our own worst enemy. People striving for
wealth and status are prisoners of their own desires.
They are ruled by an unmerciful tyrant. The more we
cater to our desires, the more they increase. The more
we get, the more we want.

We must pity the people who are slaves to their ap-
petites, who are all wrapped up in themselves, who
cannot transcend the gratification of their desires.
They want things they cannot have so much it prevents them from enjoying all they already have. Consider the addict, the person absorbed in cosmetics and
appearance, the pleasure seeker. "Just a few steps
more, then I will stop." But the further they go, the
less ability they have to resist their destruction. They
are dominated by their passions.

The control of our desires is essential to freedom.
The liberated person is self-disciplined, not self-indul-
gent. The good life is not necessarily the easiest way.
Discipline is necessary. Helen and Scott Nearing, pio-
neers in simple living, state the case for discipline.[3]

. . . the value of doing something does not lie in the
ease or difficulty, the probability or improbability of

[2]Eberhard Arnold, *Poems* (Rifton, N.Y.: Plough Publishing
[3]Helen and Scott Nearing, *Living the Good Life* (Harborside,
Maine: Social Science Institute, 1954), p. 197.
House, 1970), pp. 18-19.

its achievement, but in the vision, the plan, the determination and the perseverance, the effort and the struggle which go into the project. Life is enriched by aspiration and effort, rather than by acquisition and accumulation.

Liberation means not only freedom *from*, but freedom *for*. Living free from the controls of an economic system gives one the freedom to do what is important. Because one is not tied to what is, the status quo can be rejected. Because we are free, we can give and share. The less absorbed we are in our own comfort and security, the more we will be able to be concerned for others, and the more concerned for others we are, the less absorbed we will be in our own comfort and security.

To live simply gives one the freedom to accept jobs that are important and fulfilling but pay much less salary. One's life is released for doing significant things. Simplicity gives increased freedom of speech. One can act without fear of losing things if one has little to lose. There is no fear of being sued, having one's property confiscated, or being unable to make the payments. One is free to act boldly.

If we are free, we can live with joy and spontaneity. Singleness of purpose is not an obsession. Simplicity is spontaneous. Not needing to calculate what others may think, we can act out of integrity and freedom.

The more we live in the freedom of simplicity, the less concerned we need be about the future. We will be less shaken by a change in position, health, or fortune. Any change in these outer things does not affect the foundation of one living simply. Such a person is better prepared for struggle, adversity, or tragedy. There is more freedom to undergo repression and hardship in the quest for liberation. We are free to give and share.

CHAPTER 8

A Caring, Sharing Community

A RADICAL CHRISTIAN VISION MAKES SENSE only in the context of community. The kingdom of God is in itself a communal concept. But it is more than a concept; it is a reality to be lived now. The kingdom was never intended to be lived individually. That would be to deny its social reality. Self-seeking individualism is the opposite of the life-style of the kingdom.

Love is not exclusive. It seeks others. We are social animals and find our humanity through relationships. To desire independence is to want to be separated from God and from our brothers and sisters. The result is we fear our neighbors as ourselves instead of loving them as ourselves. We were never meant to be isolated from each other.

Christian values are inseparable from small communities of people who have committed their lives to each other. Radical Christianity from the early church down to the present has always found community to be an integral part of its life. Community is a natural outgrowth of the Christian vision.

I need my brothers and sisters to help me be a Christian.

They are important for my liberation. I cannot even be human by myself. Community is neither a luxury or window dressing. It is a necessity. The radical Christian cannot exist without community. It is necessary for spiritual and sometimes even physical survival. Our spirits tend to dry up if we allow ourselves to be isolated from others. If we go along with the values of society, survival is not a problem (except when Babylon finally falls). But if we reject those values, we must find other means of survival. If we move in the direction suggested in this book we will receive the wrath of the old sick society. What we are talking about is too threatening to the fragile old structures. But there is no discipleship without the cross.

So the question is how to refuse to be a part of the system and yet survive. We cannot go it alone. We need support. Often we know what we need to do but fear to do it. We need support to overcome our fears. The continual propaganda barrages from the media cause us to doubt our inner feelings about what the good life is. We need support from others to strengthen us. Tyrants can rule effectively only over people who are isolated from each other. Individualism is used to divide, weaken, and separate people from each other. We need community to sustain us in the struggle.

We need community to help us discern what we should be doing. Economic choices are not always easy and we need help from others to guide us. We need a community against which we can check our leadings. We do not find truth by ourselves, but in struggle with our brothers and sisters. It is in community that the guidance of the Spirit is finally discerned. When a whole community turns toward the light, we can trust its decision more than that of any individual, for it is in the context of community that the Spirit moves most freely. And as that community searches, many new ideas will come that one would not have recieved by oneself.

We need community for discipline and correction. It is difficult for us to decide individually what we need and do not need. It is too easy for us to rationalize. We need criticism of self. We need to confront each other with where our commitments lie. When the revolution comes, dope will not grow on trees and there will not be continual sex in the streets. The new life is not everyone doing their own thing and not caring about others. Self-indulgence does not lead to liberation. Discipline in the context of community can be liberating. It is founded on unity with one's brothers and sisters and grows out of love for them. It is self-imposed. Authoritarianism is discipline from outside.

We need community to help us change. Before we can convincingly talk about changing society we need to begin making those changes in our own lives. The support of a community challenges us and gives us courage to change. One cannot seriously be a part of a group of people deeply committed to each other without undergoing deep changes, changes that affect one's total life. When we see ourselves as others see us we cannot remain unchanged. When we see the potential of life in community we cannot be satisfied with the old society. Within community the revolution is taking place. There the kingdom is breaking in and lives are being changed.

The structures of our society have a fantastic influence upon us. In community we can begin to create new structures that will have more influence upon our lives than all the old structures. A community that lives by a new reality provides us with a new context and definition of sanity, a place to stand where we do not need to be on the defensive. There new relationships can emerge which will be more powerful than the system. But to be more powerful than the old system, our power cannot be on the same base as the old. Our new life will find its power on a base that the old structures can not touch.

We need community to fulfill needs and dreams that our consumer society cannot fill. As our emptiness is filled in community, the consumerism in us can be eliminated. In community we can find identity, trust, and love. Community can be a constant source of acceptance, reconciliation, courage, and hope. There we can overcome the psychic scarcity of our society and find healing for our broken lives. There we can receive affection and find joy. Unless our own needs are cared for we will never be able to care for others. Community gives us the power to move out with love to others. There we can merge the personal with the political.

We need community in raising children. Not only do we need support and love; our children need it too. But community is also important in how we raise them. If we are in community there is no need for us to force any of our values upon our children. They will be able to see them as a living reality and can decide for themselves if they will choose them. Community can provide additional means of sharing between children and adults and with other children. Rather than helping children adjust to society, it can help provide them the freedom to say either yes or no to society. Community can provide an island of freedom for our children in the midst of oppression.

If the old society is sick, we need community to experiment with new alternatives. Community is the context in which to do it. It can provide an alternative to the sterility of contractual and compulsory relationships. It can begin to relate to the problem of a disintegrating family structure and become a liberated zone where the new can emerge. There we can begin to experience already what we are working toward. We can begin building new social expressions of our faith. We can build new relationships from the bottom up. Community begins to make credible the new reality God is creating.

We need community to serve as a prophetic voice. It is an emphatic NO in the midst of the old society. But it is also a YES, a powerful sign pointing to the new. The center of power in society is in creating something new. This is not only subversive, but has also tremendous power for renewal. Community is the embodiment of the new.

We have been discussing the importance of community, but have not defined it.

There is no one shape that community needs to take. All we will say is that it is a group of people who have committed and share their lives with each other. There is no one form this must take. It can mean a group getting together once a week for deep sharing or it can mean living together. Community does not refer to casual groups where there is no commitment.

Community is more than commitment to other people. It is the result of a common commitment. Only those communities with a religious base, with a common purpose and focus beyond themselves, exist for very long. Unity on goals and methods is not enough for a successful community. There must be something deeper than this shared by all. The community that exists for itself turns in on itself and dies. To survive a group must have a goal more important than itself, something worth sacrificing for and express a concern for others not a part of the community.

Although there can be no community without a collective commitment, personal freedom is also important. Without a voluntary commitment on the part of each person a community can become a tyranny. There needs to be a balance between the personal and collective. True community does not stifle persons, but stimulates each person to greater integrity and creativity.

There can be little community unless its members are honest with each other. The truth is spoken in love. Genuineness of community is tested by the ability of its members to criticize each other and the community itself without being alienated from the community. Hurts, aggravations, and doubts need to be expressed in addition to joy, love, and faith. In community nothing can be hidden. All feelings eventually come out or else destroy the community.

Community must come to terms with the reality of human sin, a problem which can be compounded in community life. Not all communities are good. The KKK, Mafia, and even many religious communities have become an expression of the human problem rather than an answer to it. For this reason it is very important to have something beyond the group to bring judgment on it, to pull it toward the truth. Transcendence is needed. For a Christian community, this is Christ. The life of the Christian community is always measured by His Lordship.

Community is a gift, not something we create. It is similar to love. We do not create love, but become open to loving others. That is not to say that love does not involve struggle and much hard work. But love is a gift. Don't join a community on principle. Don't start with any hardened ideas of what community should be. Rather, begin to open your own life to the inbreaking of a new reality. Be open to surprises. Begin to share deeply with others and allow community to develop where there is opportunity. Be aware of where and how the Spirit has been working in other groups. You will receive vision and courage from them and you may even be led to one of them. Open your life to God's Spirit and to your sisters and brothers.

It is difficult to imagine a very deep community without some form of economic sharing. That may mean only helping those who are in need, or it may mean holding everything in common. There is no question that to begin to commit ourselves to others and share economically will radically change our relationship to them. Why not also share our lives in this way? A minimum in this area would seem to be to open all our financial secrets to the group and be examined by them. If we tell these things to the tax collector, why not to our sisters and brothers? It is also difficult to imagine a community in which some live more luxuriously than others.

Community is a new way of relating to each other.

This includes a new approach to power, leadership, and decision making. There is little similarity to bureaucratic and authoritarian relationships. Decisions are made by consensus, not hierarchically. The Quakers have been practicing this for hundreds of years and it does work.[1] This non-authoritarian approach to leadership and decision-making checks one person from running a group or a group overrunning one person. Each member is a responsible person who is totally accepted by all the others.

Consensus is not something arrived at through compromise or sensitivity, but a gift that comes to us from God. It is based on openness to the guidance of the Spirit. This is one of the basic reasons secular communes fail. They do not have an adequate basis for decision making. They rely too much on their own ideas or those of a leader.

From a Christian perspective, decisions are not worked out according to our interests, but in relation to God. Only this approach can lead to a truly decentralized society. God is still leading His movement. A Christian community recognizes His leadership among His people and they allow Him to guide them. Thus business meetings become meetings for worship. More reliance is put on the leading of the Spirit than on rhetoric. A decision is made only as people feel comfortable with the decision. Often the more people struggle to agree the more they stand in the way of God bringing them together. The life of the community literally depends upon its reliance on the Spirit to guide it.

Community can be open only to those who are

---

[1]This is also practiced by many communal groups, including the Society of Brothers (Bruderhof) in Rifton, New York, and Reba Place Fellowship in Evanston, Illinois. Anyone interested in Christian communities may want to contact these groups. My association with both of these groups has had a deep impact on my life.

serious about changing their lives. It requires a total commitment to a radical reorientation of one's values and life-style. It is open only to those who are searching for a new life.

CHAPTER 9

Jesus: Our President and Our Chairman

TO SEEK FIRST THE KINGDOM IS TO FOLLOW Jesus, to do what he said and live the life-style to which he pointed. Christian faith is a way of life, not a method of worship or a set of propositions to be believed. One's faith is expressed in the way one lives. The Gospel is not to be intellectualized, but lived.

A Christian style of life is an attempt to adopt a form of social life that conforms to the gospel. We have no lord or ruler but Jesus. He is our President and our Chairman. The result is a life-style lived in faithfulness to Him rather than to the other powers around us.

Jesus is the Christ who revealed the nature of truth and reality and God's will for humanity. Because of this, Jesus' teachings are taken seriously. If Jesus is the definition of reality, then anything that contradicts that reality is ultimately unrealistic. All the compromises made in the name of "realism" are unrealistic. Jesus Christ is reality. Those who are in control of the present power structures are captives of illusions.

All that Jesus said and did must be seen in the context of his apocalyptic vision. Jesus was aware that a new age is breaking into the present that will overthrow the existing order and establish a new order of reality. He knew that a new outpouring of the Spirit was imminent. This new age is the kingdom of God, God's rule upon earth. All of Jesus' concerns were related to this coming age.

This new reality was seen as much more than a rearrangement of old priorities or a different method of conceptualizing social problems. The change he talked

165

of was much deeper than even a new consciousness, more permanent and stable than the age of Aquarius. This new age is a totally new reality which breaks into the present from beyond the present order. It is that reality which is the center of history and is even now in the process of actualization.

The important debate today is not between liberals and conservatives, socialists and capitalists, left and right, but between the old age and the new. It is between those who are still committed to the structures of the old age and those who have been grasped by a new vision. Because of the new, the old becomes quite insignificant. One lives with passion in the new.

Jesus was therefore not interested in improvement of present society. His faith was not in the world system, but in its Maker. He saw no point in trying to restructure what is coming to an end. There is no evidence that Jesus was interested in reforming the Roman Empire. To recognize that God is in control is to understand that everything does not depend on us. We do not have to solve all the world's problems, but we can be open to God working through us. With this attitude we will probably solve some of them.

How tragic it is that people who call themselves Christians give their lives to defend, protect, maintain and support the structures of the old age. There is no hope for Babylon. Babylon is going to fall (Revelation 18:1–19:3). Why waste our lives trying to preserve it? Why give our lives to maintain it? It is passing away. If we refuse to leave Babylon, then we will fall with it.

It is important to realize that to continue in the present order will lead to our own ruin. Although we can not predict what the future holds or how the old order will collapse, we can act in the faith that the new somehow by God's grace will replace the old. Our concern is to act faithfully in the new order. We can break our commitments and loyalties to the old order. We can say a clear no to all sin. We do not need to support it any longer.

Neither did Jesus have any illusions about humanity being able to save itself. He knew that people by their own effort would never get themselves out of the mess they are in. He had no concept of progress. He understood that humanity's attempt to better itself is really an attempt to make itself god and can be expected to result in alienation not only from God, but from our neighbors and ourselves.

Those things (*e.g.*, pollution) which now threaten human existence are the results of our attempt to better ourselves and will continue until our lives are drastically changed. Our attempt to save ourselves leads to death because it involves cutting ourselves off from the source of life and healing.

Jesus' vision of the kingdom was not otherworldly, however. It was very much related to this world. The kingdom is at hand *here*, not some place else. It is directly related to the current issues of life. That is why Jesus talked so much about economics. It may not be *of* the world, but it is very much *in* the world. God is at work in his world today.

Jesus' statement that if his kingdom were of this world, then his followers would fight (John 18:36) means just what it says. If his kingdom were *of* the old order, then he would struggle for power to reform the old structures. He did not say the kingdom is unrelated to the present world. In fact, he called people to begin changing their lives (repent) to prepare for it. That includes social action, but based on hope in the new age rather than in the old. The kingdom relates directly to the present. We are to begin living in it now.

Such theology obviously will lead to a radically new life-style based on expectancy and anticipation of something new.

It will mean radically reorienting our lives toward the coming of the kingdom. We will begin to make decisions not on the ordinary evidence of history, but on the basis of something new we see coming.

This means nonconformity to the society around us. Paul wrote, "Do not be comformed to this world but be transformed by the renewal of your mind" (Romans 12:2). Paul understood that the structures of the old age were in direct conflict with the new reality. The Christian faith (not the culture-religion proclaimed in most churches) is as radical a criticism of our culture as it was of first century culture.

Bourgeois American life is incompatible with following Jesus. The new reality that Jesus calls us to is practically the opposite of what our society expects of us. Many of the values of our society stand in direct contradiction to those of the Bible. Materialism is just one example. There is a fundamental antagonism between the children of light and the children of darkness. Peace with God means conflict with the world. The desire for respectability really is not Christian.

The reason so many people consider Jesus' teachings to be impractical is that they demand we change our lives. They do not give us sanction to continue our normal path. Too many Christians want to be like the world and be respected by it. They want to live in Canaan and enjoy the goodies of Babylon. But it is impossible to live according to the old order and remain faithful to the new. To the extent we live in the old age, we do not participate in the new age. Those who thought they could serve two masters have ended up with watered down churches with no spiritual power, preaching not the kingdom, but pagan American culture religion.

We are pilgrims. We have no permanent city. We live in a foreign land. We live with expectation. We cannot cling to the past, for a new reality is always upon us. We are called to live in the present. Those who fight always fight about past conceptions.

A note must be made here concerning the strong thrust of psychology to equate adjustment with health.

Maladjustments have been considered problems of the individual. But maybe they point to problems in the society. To be well adjusted in a sick society is really to be sick.

Christianity is expressed in the form of a counter culture.

The Jesus movement was not about building the new age through social and economic reform, but calling people into a new (redeemed) community which would begin to concretize the coming of the new age. The coming of God's rule was to be already realized in a new historical community, a new people.

Jesus began a new movement whose goal was a new social order, the kingdom of God. This was not to be created by His followers, but was to become a reality in their midst as they began to participate in God's creation of the new. His followers were the new people of God. John Miller, a founder of Reba Place Fellowship, writes that Jesus expected

> . . . that out of His work a movement would arise, a people who would live together in the spirit of a close and loving family. In the context of this community, the man who left all to follow Jesus would find a new sphere of economic and social support. . . . Though buffeted by persecutions and trials of various kinds the needs of the disciples would be met . . . *by a loving God working through a generous people.* That is Jesus' vision of economic life among his disciples.[1]

Jesus proclaimed the year of Jubilee (Luke 4:18-19). The year of Jubilee was commanded (Leviticus 25) by God to be practiced by the Hebrews every fiftieth year. This is an extension of the sabbatical year which came every seventh year. In the year of Jubilee,

---

[1]John W. Miller, *The Christian Way* (Scottdale, Pa.: Herald Press, 1969), pp. 87-88.

all debts were to be canceled, all slaves freed and the wealth redistributed.

The early church as well as groups like the Hutterites developed a theology of Jubilee, held everything in common and developed new forms of social organization. The early Christian community was a counter culture living the Jubilee.[2] Note the Biblical description of that community.

> Now the company of those who believed were of one heart and soul, and no one said that any of the things which he possessed was his own, but they had everything in common. And with great power the apostles gave their testimony to the resurrection of the Lord Jesus, and great grace was upon them all. There was not a needy person among them, for as many as were possessors of lands or houses sold them, and brought the proceeds of what was sold and laid it at the apostles' feet; and distribution was made to each as any had need. *Acts 4:32-35*

The unique and powerful aspect of the early Christian communities was not only their teaching, but the quality of their new life. That is why they not only survived, but became the stabilizing force in a crumbling empire and society. They practiced love and service. Forgiveness, justice, and reconciliation were realities in their lives. In a country where class distinctions were rigid, they practiced equality regardless of class, race, or wealth. No one was allowed to dominate others. Sharing was a concrete concern with people taking personal responsibility for each other.

Christianity is not expressed as only one life-style or cultural form, but it is always expressed as a cultural form. One cannot divorce Christian faith from its concrete expression even though it can never be identified with that expression. No one cultural form can be

---

[2]For those interested in the life-style of the early church, see Eberhard Arnold, *The Early Christians* (Rifton, N.Y.: Plough Publishing House, 1970).

called *the* Christian life-style, but there are many life-styles that are definitely not Christian.

One of the main tests given to the church today is whether the Christian faith has the power to create a new style of life in the midst of the chaos of the old. Many church people at most receive emotional support from the activities of the church rather than those activities being an expression of a new reality that already exists.

Wherever disciples of Jesus live, their life together will demonstrate a new attitude toward life, both in relation to God and the needs of others. Because they are no longer slaves of Mammon, but liberated to a new life, they will live without anxiety, sharing their possessions with one another and the needy everywhere. They will be known for their unselfishness, generosity, and sharing. They will be sowing the seeds of a new society.

To become a part of this new community, this Christian counter culture, one must be willing to give up all.

Jesus said, "Whoever of you does not renounce all that he has cannot be my disciple" (Luke 14:33). That means everything, even our egos. No more ego trips. Discipleship is costly. Jesus even asked the woman caught in adultery to give up her livelihood (John 8:1-11). It means giving up all, including our ambitions, and seeking only to do God's will. Only those who lose their lives will save them.

> If any man would come after me, let him deny himself and take up his cross daily and follow me. For whoever would save his life will lose it; and whoever loses his life for my sake, he will save it.   *Luke 9:23,24.*

Jesus demonstrated this new attitude in His own life. Jesus was born poor, shared all that He had, and died poor. "Foxes have holes, and birds of the air have nests; but the Son of man has nowhere to lay his head" (Matthew 8:20).

The Christian faith is not based on regalia and majesty, but upon Christ who emptied himself of his divine glory and humbled himself by becoming a servant (Philippians 2:5-9). His lowly birth, humble upbringing, and his free life all point to a life of simplicity. Paul said,

> For you know the grace of our Lord Jesus Christ, that though he was rich, yet for your sake he became poor, so that by his poverty you might become rich.
> *2 Corinthians 8:9.*

Not wealth, but poverty is the sign of those who identify with Jesus, the one who is the companion of the poor, who will feed the hungry and send the rich empty away (Luke 1:53). Those who do not share with the needy and help them will not enter the kingdom (Matthew 25:31-46).

Christian renunciation is not escape from the world, but a new way of living in it. It is not an ascetic denial of the world, but the fine dialectic of living *in* the world, but not *of* it. The Christian puts the kingdom first. Everything else is secondary. Creation is not denied, but seen in a new light. The kingdom brings the fragmented pieces all together again.

One of the most important aspects of life is the economic, whether that be earning a living, consuming, or relating to others personally or corporately.

If you want to know what people really consider important, listen not to what they say, but see how they use their money. Because of the centrality of Christ and the incarnation, the Christian is most concerned about the point where the material world and the transcendent meet. The Christian stands there at that point and feels the tension of the two.

It is crucial that we deal with economics from a Christian perspective because this question has been for the most part ignored. The predominant ethic is strict individualism in regard to wealth. What Christians do with their wealth has been considered their private business. The church, friends, and even the Christian faith are expected to keep out of this area. It is a subject one does not discuss with friends. Complete secrecy shrouds our private economic life. We tend to be even more sensitive about our economic life than our sex life. Why? Is it because there is so much guilt here?

It is simply not true, as some contend, that Jesus did not address himself to economic questions. Actually, in the Gospels Jesus addresses himself more often to economic issues than to any other question. The Bible is as clear on the question of economics as any subject. The injunctions against economic exploitation and accumulation of wealth are completely unambiguous.

Consider the Levitical codes concerning the treatment of the poor or Jesus' command to not lay up treasures on earth. We cannot dismiss Jesus' words about the rich fool, Dives, and the eye of a needle. For the Christian, the issue of money and possessions was settled long ago. The economic process is not autonomous or an end in itself, but must be brought under the Lordship of Christ. The Bible is concerned with both inner motivation and the outward details of daily living.

If Jesus, living in a more simple society, showed so much concern with money, how much more do we need to see this as a critical area for faithfulness? Some argue that Jesus made sense then, but not today. Actually His teachings were just as unreasonable to the materialist then as now.

It is not true that the way of Jesus is possible only in an agrarian society. It is even more relevant now as we are destroying ourselves. Jesus Christ cannot be dismissed so easily. Those who have taken his teachings on economic life seriously have not found them to be impractical or utopian. They are part of the vision he had of what it means for people to live by the will of God.

We now turn to the Biblical understanding of property.[3]

The understanding that all that is belongs to God is basic. "The earth is the Lord's and the fulness thereof" (Psalm 24:1). Instead of thinking of ourselves as owners, we should see ourselves as stewards and trustees. All that is belongs to God and has been given to us as a public trust. A Christian cannot say, "This is mine and I will do with it as I please." Only an atheist may make that statement. Nor will the Christian accept stewardship of possessions unjustly obtained, that should not come under our control.

The idea of private property has its roots in the individualistic notion that each person is by nature self-sufficient and sovereign. The Bible clearly rejects this idea. The individualistic idea of private property is not biblical. The Hebrew prophets were very critical of Israel when she reverted back to the competitive, individualistic economy of the surrounding heathen nations. This included the practice of slavery and failure to regularly redistribute the wealth (the year of Jubilee).

Property in the Old Testament, while often held by an individual, was owned by the family, clan, or com-

---

[3]For an excellent discussion of the biblical view of property and economic relations, see Peter Walpot, "Concerning True Surrender and Christian Community of Goods," *Mennonite Quarterly Review*, XXXI (January, 1957), pp. 5-45. A reprint is available from Plough Publishing House, Rifton, N.Y. This early Hutterite work is a moving statement of a radical Christian view of economics.

munity. It could not be sold at will. One could not do with property as one pleased and amass wealth for oneself without consideration of others. Detailed rules were given for the relation of the whole community to property. Interest and usury were forbidden and lending to those in need was considered a duty.

The word wealth appears many times in the Bible, sometimes in a positive sense, sometimes negative. The book of Proverbs especially sees it as positive. Although there are repeated warnings concerning the dangers of wealth, there is no call for complete rejection of things. It is made clear, however, that all wealth must be totally subordinate to God's will.

While the Bible talks much about the goodness of creation, there is also a clear warning against accumulation of wealth which is seen as a challenge to the Lordship of God and a sign of mistrust of God. Isaiah pronounced woe on all who add house to house and field to field (Isaiah 5:8). Solomon is rebuked for his accumulation of wealth. Deuteronomy warns against the dangers of a settled life.

The Bible sees affluence as evil whenever it leads to a rejection of one's dependence upon God or when it was obtained at the expense of another person. Abundance is something rather to enjoy than to hoard and accumulate. The Hebrews escaping Egypt could daily gather manna, but they were not allowed to store any of it.

There is no hint in the Bible that the material world is evil or inferior. The Bible affirms the goodness of creation. "And God saw everything that he had made, and behold, it was very good" (Genesis 1:31). The Bible is not ascetic. God promised Israel a land flowing with milk and honey. Abundance is part of the glory of creation. "If you are willing and obedient, you shall eat the good of the land" (Isaiah 1:19).⁴

Possessions are not evil. There is a problem, howev-

---

⁴Also see Deuteronomy 8:7-10.

er, with the perverted will of humanity, with our refusal to see things in their relation to God's purpose. People take what is good and by using it for selfish interests set demonic forces in motion. Exploitation, envy, suspicion, and alienation result. The love of money is the root of all evils (1 Timothy 6:10). Things are good, but our slavery to them has denied us freedom, spontaneity and relationships. What was meant for good has become our downfall.

Greed may be a denial of the goodness of creation because, rather than accept creation for what it is, we feel the need to give it value by making it exclusively our own. Perhaps we consider it less good if it is not in our possession. This is to set ourselves up as God, the Creator, rather than to see other created things as having value because God created them.

The best way to affirm the goodness of creation is to use it properly and give all people equal access and rightful stewardship responsibilities to it. This means good stewardship of what has been given to us, conservation, and non-exploitation. One treats the environment with respect and therefore does not waste or pollute it. It means taking care of what we have and not accumulating more than we can take care of. An affirmation of the goodness of creation leads to a passionate concern for economic and social justice.

We have seen how the material creation is good and that property has a place within the community. The philosophy of materialism is nowhere accepted in the Bible, however. The assumption is never made that all of reality is material or measurable. The desire for wealth implies a worship of those things and rebellion against God. The tenth commandment—against covetousness—is to be taken seriously. The inner desire leads not only to stealing and oppression, but also to idolatry (Colossians 3:5). The more one seeks after material things, the more alienated one is from God. The materialist's faith is not in God, but in possessions. "If riches increase, set not your heart on them" (Psalm 62:10).

Jesus was especially dogmatic in denouncing riches. He unmasked the sickness of the propertied classes and showed them for what they are. For Him it was a question of identity and loyalty. "Where your treasure is, there will your heart be also" (Matthew 6:21). He did not say your heart should not be there, but that it will be.

Jesus' attitude toward property was basically not an ascetic renunciation, but a call to leave all for something greater. He declared war on the spirit of materialism and implied that all His followers would be part of that struggle. Jesus used the term "mammon" (Aramaic for wealth) to describe money. Mammon has demonic connotations and points to wealth as a rival of God. Jesus said,

> No servant can serve two masters; for either he will hate the one and love the other, or he will be devoted to the one and despise the other. You cannot serve God and mammon. *Luke 16:13.*

Jesus did not say that one should not serve two masters. He said it is impossible. Mammon is in rebellion against God and competes for our loyalty and allegiance. It is in direct opposition to the rule of God. Mammon is not neutral. Wealth in itself is not evil, but wealth as a god (mammon) is to be resisted. All of us must deal with the mammon spirit. It is part of the massive struggle with the principalities and powers. The god Mammon is to be overthrown.

Jesus did not say that it would be impossible for a rich person to enter the kingdom, but He did say it would be extremely difficult.

> How hard it is for those who have riches to enter the kingdom of God! For it is easier for a camel to go through the eye of a needle than for a rich man to enter the kingdom of God. *Luke 18:24,25.*

It can happen only by God's grace. Jesus told the rich young ruler that he would have to give everything away before he could enter the kingdom. His attachment to his possessions kept him out.

Jesus reversed the whole approach to economics. Society says that it is better to have more than less. A thousand dollars is better than a hundred dollars. But is it? One of the basic values of western civilization is that a person has the right to amass private wealth and do with it as one pleases. This, however, is directly counter to Jesus' command, "Do not lay up for yourselves treasures on earth" (Matthew 6:19).

Not only is this an expression of private, individualistic morality which denies corporate responsibility, but it also keeps one from entering the new community. When God's will is done, both poverty and wealth disappear. The Christian seeks to avoid accumulating possessions instead of striving for them. The Christian deliberately does not become wealthy. One gives up all claim to everything, for everything belongs to God.

The eighteenth chapter of Revelation is a dramatic description of the fall of Babylon and the old age. A detailed description of the city's luxury items shows that wealth is an intricate part of the evil of the city. When Babylon falls, the businessmen along with all their luxury items and wealth are overthrown.

The Bible challenges almost every economic value of our society.

The Bible also has much to say about poverty.

For the most part, the Bible sees the cause of poverty being greed, war, deceit, and oppression of the masses by the rich. Jesus' statement that the poor will always be with us is no denial of this. Poverty is not a natural part of the world, but the result of the sin of oppression and injustice by those in power.

The book of Proverbs is a partial exception to this, but even Proverbs shows distrust for wealth. "He who trusts in his riches will wither" (Proverbs 11:28). It also counsels compassion for the poor. Those who blame poverty on the poor and say it is a result of their sin have not taken the Bible seriously.

The Bible is prejudiced against the rich and for the poor. To a large extent wealth is seen as coming from the oppression of the poor. Except in a few places, riches are not praised and the wealthy are not seen as a good example. The rich are often shown to be suffering from spiritual poverty. Jesus said,

> But woe to you that are rich, for you have received your consolation. Woe to you that are full now, for you shall hunger. *Luke 6:24,25.*

God is shown to be sympathetic to the poor. "He raises up the poor from the dust; he lifts the needy from the ash heap" (1 Samuel 2:8). Jesus said, "Blessed are you poor, for yours is the kingdom of God" (Luke 6:20). Jesus came for the poor and promised the kingdom to them. Jesus himself was the poor man par excellence. Often the poor are equated with the righteous.

> Has not God chosen those who are poor in the world to be rich in faith and heirs of the kingdom which he has promised to those who love him? But you have dishonored the poor man. Is it not the rich who oppress you, is it not they who drag you into court?
> *James 2:5-7.*

It has been suggested that the poor are those who have nothing invested in the status quo. That should be also a mark of the Christian.

The rights of the poor are upheld in the Bible. They are not commanded to protect the wealth of the rich, but the rich are commanded to protect the rights of the poor. In Hebrew society, the fate of the poor was not left to chance or those rare moments when the prosperous might feel sympathy and offer token charity. Many laws guaranteed the rights of the poor and outlined the responsibilities of the prosperous toward them. (See Deuteronomy 15:1-11) For example, the poor had a right to go into the fields to gather food and not be guilty of theft. The farmers were required to leave some of the crop in the field for the poor (Deuteronomy 23:24,25).

Charity for the poor was not a privilege defined by society, but a right granted by God. Sharing with the poor is based not on our kindness, but on God's love and mercy for all of us.

Today, we deal with the poor in many ways. We give them welfare, preach patience to them, and degrade them. The Bible demands justice for them.

God has not forgotten the poor, the diseased, the oppressed. He sends people to serve them. Sometimes he needs to take people of strength and wealth, break them of their pride and unreasonableness, and send them out to do what must be done. If only we would accept God's will voluntarily instead of being broken to it.

The Christian is called to stand with the oppressed, to "maintain the rights of the poor and needy" (Proverbs 31:9). Jesus said that whatever you do to one of the least of these you do to Him. (Matthew 25:10). This is the basis of the last judgment. Today Christ is to be found among the poor, the destitute, the homeless, the prisoners. If we want to meet Christ, that is where He is.

Those who would live the new life must enter it on faith, totally trusting God.

To the extent we surround ourselves with outward securities and refuse to trust God, we are not prepared for the kingdom. Our natural tendency is to care first for our own needs and then show concern for others. But Jesus calls for just the opposite. We are first of all to love our God, seek His kingdom, and care for our brothers and sisters.

The seeking of wealth and security is a sign of unbelief in the goodness of God. Jesus said,

> Truly, I say to you, there is no one who has left house or brothers or sisters or mother or father or children or lands, for my sake and for the gospel, who will not receive a hundredfold now in this time, houses and brothers and sisters and mothers and children and lands, with persecutions, and in the age to come eternal life. *Mark 10:29,30.*

Anyone who completely trusts God and determines to do his will and follow the leading of the Spirit need never worry about the future. God will provide for us to the extent we allow Him. But so often we do not believe Jesus. Many times God does not have first place in our lives. Thoreau put it well. "How vigilant we are! determined not to live by faith if we can avoid it."[5]

Fear complicates life. Consider all the false securities that tangle us up. Trust makes these unnecessary. Faith means freedom. Those who have faith can take the risk of commitment. They can trust people even though they know they are not trustworthy. There are two types of naiveté: the kind that does not know better and the kind that does but moves ahead in simple trust.

Jesus said not to worry about tomorrow. What a profound understanding of reality. Everyone would be better off if everyone shared. The Bible is much deeper in its understanding of economics than most modern textbooks. Following the biblical way would leave no one hungry. The failure to recognize that God will provide for us has led to inequality and all the suffering that goes with it.

To those who serve Mammon, this will make little

---

[5]Henry David Thoreau, *Walden* (New York: Mentor Books, 1957), p.12.

sense. They must take a materialistic view. Mammon is concerned only about profit and success, and makes no promise to the sick, the widows, the aged, and the unprofitable.

Babylon does not know the God who gives good things for all to enjoy, for the world is not seen as a gift, but as an arena of fierce struggle for survival. Therefore, the disciples of Mammon must be concerned about tomorrow and make every provision possible, for when they are no longer useful to the system, they will be discarded. Thus for them life insurance, annuities, and investments are important. The pagan system demands it.

But for the Christian it makes little sense. Why invest in what is passing away? Why put faith in western civilization? That is not security. Actually we have little control over our material existence and it is futile to worry about it. This is not to imply that there should be no rational economic planning, but it should be done on different premises. All our economic planning should be based on a quality of trust in God and the future.

We must be willing to leave the old way of life for a new one we do not yet see or understand. Yes, it is foolish, but it is no more foolish than for a Columbus to start out on his ill-advised journey to the edge of the earth. If we are unsatisfied with the old and are grasped by the new, we can do no other.

Those who trust God can venture out, knowing that God will be there in the future also. "Seek first his kingdom . . . and all these things shall be yours as well." That was a promise!

Bibliography

Arnold, Eberhard. *Salt and Light*. Tr. Society of Brothers. Rifton, New York: Plough Publishing House, 1967, pp. 75-160.

Arnold, Eberhard. *The Early Christians*. Tr. Society of Brothers. Rifton, New York: Plough Publishing House, 1970.

Aukerman, Dale. "Brethren Millionaires," *Gospel Messenger* (Church of the Brethren, CII (July 4, 1953), pp. 14-15.

Aukerman, Dale. "It's Time to De-accumulate," *Gospel Messenger*, CXIII (February 1, 1964), pp. 18-20.

Baron, Paul A., and Sweezy, Paul M. *Monopoly Capital.* New York: Monthly Review Press, 1966.

Barclay's Apology in Modern English. Edited by Dean Freiday. Phila.: Friends Book Store, 1967, pp. 389-424.

Bauman, Clarence. "The Christian and the Economic Order." Unpublished paper in possession of author.

Berry, Wendell. *The Long-Legged House.* New York: Harcourt, Brace & World, Inc., 1969.

Blough, S. S. *Studies in Doctrine and Devotion.* Elgin, Ill.: Brethren Publishing House, 1919, pp. 174-195.

Bowman, Walter D. "The Perils of Prosperity," *Messenger* (Church of the Brethren), CXVI (February 16, 1967), pp. 5-7.

Borsodi, Ralph. *This Ugly Civilization.* New York: Harper & Brothers, 1933.

Caillet, Greg, *et al. Everyman's Guide to Ecological Living.* New York: Macmillan, 1971.

Callenbach, Ernest. *Living Poor With Style.* New York: Bantam Books, 1972.

Cornell, Thomas C., and Forest, James H. *A Penny a Copy: Readings from the Catholic Worker.* New York: Macmillan, 1968.

Croley, Victor A. "The Freedom Way," *Mother Earth News.* I (January, 1970), pp. 46-55.

Davis, Adelle. *Let's Eat Right to Keep Fit.* New York: Harcourt, 1954.

Day, Dorothy. *Loaves and Fishes.* New York: Harper & Row, 1963.

Deo, Shankarrao. *Could We not Agree on Gandhi's Alternative to Capitalism.* Thanjavur: Sarvodaya Prachuralaya, 1969.

Dickinson, Richard. "So Who Needs Liberation?" *Christian Century,* LXXXVIII (January 13, 1971), pp. 43-46.

The Ecology and Politics Manual. Edited by Alan S. Miller and Phil Farnham. Available from 491 Guerrero St., San Francisco, 94110.

Eddy, Sherwood. *Religion and Social Justice.* New York: George H. Doran Co., 1927, pp. 9-127.

Eller, Vernard. *Kierkegaard and Radical Discipleship.* Princeton, New Jersey: Princeton University Press, 1968, pp. 213-259.

Ellul, Jacques. *The Meaning of the City.* Tr. Dennis Pardee. Grand Rapids, Michigan: Eerdmans, 1970.

Ellul, Jacques, *The Presence of the Kingdom.* Tr. Olive Wyon. New York: Seabury Press, 1967.

Ellul, Jacques. *The Technological Society.* Tr. John Wilkinson. New York: Vintage Books, 1964.

Eshelman, Matthew M. *Nonconformity to the World.* Dayton, Ohio: Christian Publishing Association, 1874.

Fager, Charles E. *The Window in the Tower: An Essay on the Ancient Quaker Testimony of Simplicity.* 1970. Unpublished manuscript in the Haverford College Library.

Faw, William. "The Bible Blesses the Poor," *Messenger,* CXIX (January 3, 1970), pp. 5-7.

Fleming, Daniel Johnson. *Ventures in Simpler Living.* New York: International Missionary Council, 1933.

Florand, Francis. *Stages of Simplicity.* Tr. Sister M. Carina. St. Louis: B. Herder Book Co., 1967.

Fosdick, Harry Emerson. *The Meaning of Service.* Boston: Pilgrim Press, 1920.

Frankl, Viktor E. *Man's Search for Meaning.* New York: Washington Square Press, 1959.

Galbraith, John Kenneth. *The Affluent Society.* New York: Mentor Books, 1958.

Gandhi, M. K. *Gift of Gold.* Ahmedabad: Navajivan Publishing House, 1963.

Gandhi, M. K. *The Gospel of Renunciation.* Ahmedabad:
Navajivan Publishing House, 1961.
Gandhi, M. K. *Voluntary Poverty.* Ahmedabad: Navajivan
Publishing House, 1961.
Gibbons, Euell. *Stalking the Wild Asparagus.* New York:
David McKay, 1962.
Goodman, Paul. "Growing up Absorbed," *Liberation,* IX
(April, 1963), pp. 16-17.
Goulet, Denis. *The Cruel Choice: A New Concept in the
Theory of Development.* New York: Atheneum, 1971.
Goulet, Denis A. "The United States: A Case of Anti-
development," *Motive,* XXX (January, 1970), pp. 6-13.
Goulet, Denis A. "Voluntary Austerity: The Necessary Art,"
The Christian Century, LXXXIII (June 8, 1966), pp.
748-752.
Gray, J. Glenn. *On Understanding Violence Philosophically
and Other Essays.* New York: Harper Torchbooks, 1970,
pp. 45-68.
Gregg, Richard B. *The Value of Voluntary Simplicity*
(Pamphlet #3). Wallingford, Pa.: Pendle Hill Pamphlets,
1936.
Hall, Bolton. *Even As You and I.* London: The Simple Life
Press, 1903.
Harris, John. *Mammon.* Boston: Gould, Kendall & Lincoln,
1837.
Havens, Teresina Rowell. *Standards of Success* (Pamphlet
#43). Wallingford, Pa.: Pendle Hill Pamphlets, 1948.
Hershberger, Guy Franklin. *The Way of the Cross in Hu-
man Relations.* Scottdale, Pa.: Herald Press, 1958.
Holy Bible.
Hyma, Albert. *Christianity, Capitalism and Communism.*
Ann Arbor, Michigan: George Wahr, 1937.
The Journal of John Woolman and *A Plea for the Poor.* The
John Greenleaf Whittier Edition. New York: Corinth
Books, 1961.
Juenger, Friedrich Georg. *The Failure of Technology.* Tr.
F. D. Wieck. Hinsdale, Ill.: Henry Regnery Company,
1949.
Kagawa, Toyohiko. *Brotherhood Economics.* New York:
Harper & Brothers, 1936.
Katona, George. *The Mass Consumption Society.* New
York: McGraw-Hill, 1964.

Kelly, Thomas R. A Testament of Devotion. New York: Harper & Brothers, 1941.

Klassen, Herbert. "Property: A Problem in Christian Ethics," Concern #4, Scottdale: Herald Press, 1957, pp. 42-56.

Lao-tze. The Simple Way. Tr. Walter Gorn Old: London: William Rider & Son, 1913.

Lappé, Frances Moore. Diet for a Small Planet. New York: Ballantine Books, 1971.

Leavitt, Helen. Superhighway-Superhoax. New York: Ballantine Books, 1971.

Lichtman, Richard. "Capitalism and Consumption," Socialist Revolution, I (May-June, 1970), pp. 83-96.

McLeod, Malcolm James. The Culture of Simplicity. New York: Fleming H. Revell, 1904.

Mahoney, John. "Let's Junk the Profit Motive," U. S. Catholic, XXXVII (June, 1972), pp. 14-15.

Marcuse, Herbert. An Essay on Liberation. Boston: Beacon Press, 1969.

Marcuse, Herbert. One-Dimensional Man. Boston: Beacon Press, 1968.

Marquand, John P. Point of No Return. Boston: Little, Brown & Co., 1949.

Martin, Hugh. Christ and Money. New York: George H. Doran, [n.d.]

Martin, Hugh, ed. The Practice of the Presence of God [Brother Lawrence] and Selections from The Little Flowers of St. Francis. London: SCM Press, 1956.

Meadows, Donella H., et al. The Limits to Growth. New York: Universe Books, 1972.

Miller, Arthur. Death of a Salesman. New York: The Viking Press, 1949.

Miller, Daniel W. The Meaning of Simplicity. 1946. Unpublished manuscript in Goshen College Library.

Miller, John W. "Christian Ethics and Current Economic Problems." Unpublished paper in possession of author.

Miller, R. H. The Doctrine of the Brethren Defended. Indianapolis: Printing and Publishing House Print, 1876. pp. 323-352.

Milner, Esther. The Failure of Success. New York: Exposition Press, 1959.

Moore, J. H. The New Testament Doctrines. Elgin Ill.: Brethren Publishing House, 1915, pp. 133-174.

Morgan, Arthur E. and Morgan, Lucy G. *The Economic Basis of Idealism.* Yellow Springs, Ohio: Community Service, 1934.

Morgan, Arthur E. "It Can Be Done in Economic Life," *Community Comments,* XVI (February, 1960), pp. 65-104.

Morgan, Arthur E. *The Small Community.* New York: Harper & Brothers, 1942.

Mother Earth News

Mumford, Lewis. *The Conduct of Life.* New York: Harcourt, Brace & Co., 1951, pp. 244-292.

Nearing, Helen, and Nearing, Scott. *Living the Good Life.* Harborside, Maine: Social Science Institute, 1954.

Nearing, Scott. *Man's Search for the Good Life.* Harborside, Maine: Social Science Institute, 1954.

Nelson, George. "Design, Technology, and the Pursuit of Ugliness," *Saturday Review,* LIV (October 2, 1971), pp. 22-62.

Orchard, William E. *The Way of Simplicity.* New York: E. P. Dutton & Co., 1935.

Packard, Vance. *The Hidden Persuaders.* New York: Pocket Books, 1957.

Parodi, Pierre. *The Use of Poor Means in Helping the Third World.* Tr. Elizabeth Gravalos Marshall. South Acworth: New Hampshire: Greenleaf Books, 1970.

Petry, Ray C. *Francis of Assisi.* Durham, North Carolina: Duke University Press, 1941.

Piper, Otto A. *The Christian Meaning of Money.* Englewood Cliffs, New Jersey: Prentice-Hall, 1965.

Plus, Raoul. *Simplicity.* London: Burns, Oates & Washbourne, 1950.

Ramirez, Alice Louise. *Handbook of Survival in the City.* North Hollywood, Calif.: Now Library Press, 1970.

Reich, Charles A. *The Greening of America.* New York: Bantam Books, 1970.

Rideman, Peter. *Confession of Faith.* Tr. Society of Brothers. Rifton, New York: Plough Publishing House, 1970, pp. 112-165.

Rieman, T. Wayne. "Let's Uncomplicate Our Lives," *Messenger,* CXXI (October 1, 1972), pp. 8-11.

Rieman, T. Wayne. "More! More! More!" *Messenger,* CXX (March 15, 1971), pp. 13-15.

Roszak, Theodore. *The Making of a Counter Culture.* Garden City, New York: Anchor Books, 1969.

Santmire, H. Paul. *Brother Earth: Nature, God and Ecology in Time of Crisis.* New York: Thomas Nelson, 1970.

Scudder, Vida D. *Socialism and Character.* Boston: Houghton Mifflin Co., 1912, pp. 207-272, 416-425.

Slater, Philip E. *The Pursuit of Loneliness.* Boston: Beacon Press, 1970.

Sorokin, Pitrim. *The Crisis of Our Age.* New York: E. P. Dutton & Co., 1941.

Stein, J. W. *Non-Conformity to the World, as Taught and Practiced by the Brethren or German Baptists.* Lanark, Ill.: Brethren at Work Publishing House, 1878.

Steinbeck, John. *The Winter of Our Discontent.* New York: The Viking Press, 1961.

Stewart, James S. *The Gates of New Life.* New York: Charles Scribner's Sons, 1938, pp. 211-219.

Stowell, Robert F. *Toward Simple Living.* Hartland, Vermont: Solitarian Press, 1953.

Stringfellow, William. "Money and What It Means," *Messenger,* CXV (September 15, 1966), pp. 1-4.

Suderman, Jacob. "Yticilpmis: What About Our Simple Way of Life?" *Mennonite Life,* XIV (January, 1959), pp. 3-9.

Sun Bear. *At Home in the Wilderness.* Healdsburg, Calif.: Naturegraph Publishing Co., 1968.

Tawney, R. H. *Religion and the Rise of Capitalism.* New York: Mentor Books, 1926.

Thomas A Kempis. *The Imitation of Christ.* Tr. Leo Sherley-Price. Baltimore: Penguin Books, 1952.

Thoreau, Henry David. *Walden.* New York: Mentor Books, 1957.

Toffler, Alvin. *Future Shock.* New York: Random House, 1970.

Toynbee, Arnold J. *America and the World Revolution.* New York: Oxford University Press, 1962, pp. 103-153.

Vasudevan, K. *Gandhian Economics.* Bombay: Bharatiya Vidya Bhavan, 1967.

Veblen, Thorstein. *The Theory of the Leisure Class.* New York: The Viking Press, 1899.

Vogt, Virgil. "God or Mammon," *Concern #11.* Scottdale, Pa.: Herald Press, 1963, pp. 22-58.

Wagner, Charles. *The Simple Life.* Tr. Mary Louise Hendee. New York: McClure, Phillips & Co., 1904.

Walpot, Peter. "Concerning True Surrender and Christian Community of Goods," *Mennonite Quarterly Review,* XXXI (January, 1957), pp. 5-45. Reprints available from Plough Publishing House, Rifton, New York.

Walsh, Mary Elizabeth. *The Saints and Social Work.* Silver Spring, Maryland. The Preservation of the Faith Press, 1937.

Ward, Barbara. *The Rich Nations and the Poor Nations.* New York: Norton & Co., 1962.

Ward, Harry F. *The New Social Order.* New York: Macmillan, 1919.

Watts, Alan. *The Book.* New York: Pantheon Books, 1966.

Weber, Max. *The Protestant Ethic and the Spirit of Capitalism.* Tr. Talcott Parsons. New York: Charles Scribner's Sons, 1958.

Wellock, Wilfred. *A Mechanistic or a Human Society?* Thanjavur, India: Sarvodaya Prachuralaya, 1968.

Wellock, Wilfred. *Off the Beaten Track: Adventures in the Art of Living.* Tanjore, India: Sarvodaya Prachuralaya, 1961.

Wenger, John Christian. *Separated Unto God.* Scottdale, Pa.: Mennonite Publishing House, 1951.

West, Dan, Shelly, Andrew, and Levering, Samuel. "A Call to Simple Living," *Messenger,* CXVIII (September 11, 1969), pp. 12-13.

White, Alan. *The Wheel.* New York: Harcourt, Brace & World, Inc., 1966.

Whole Earth Catalog.

Wood Heat Quarterly.

Young, Mildred Binns. *Another Will Gird You* (Pamphlet #109). Wallingford, Pa.: Pendle Hill Pamphlets, 1960.

Young, Mildred Binns. *A Standard of Living* (Pamphlet #12). Wallingford, Pa.: Pendle Hill Pamphlets, [1941].

Young, Mildred Binns. *What Doth the Lord Require of Thee?* (Pamphlet #145). Wallingford, Pa.: Pendle Hill Pamphlets, 1966.

THE AUTHOR

Art Gish was born and raised on a farm in Lancaster County, Pa. He is a graduate of Manchester College and Bethany Theological Seminary and has served as a pastor in the Church of the Brethren.

He did alternative service as a conscientious objector in Europe, working in a home for crippled teenagers and international work camps. He participated in the civil rights movement in Chicago and the Poor People's Campaign in Resurrection City. He has also been active in the peace movement.

He is the author of *The New Left and Christian Radicalism* and numerous articles and is a contributing editor of *The Other Side* and *The Post-American.*

Art, an itinerate preacher, spends much of his time traveling with his family across the country speaking to churches, colleges, and seminaries and sometimes in the streets. He is especially interested in radical Christianity and a recovery of the Anabaptist vision.

Art and his wife Peggy have two children, Dale and Daniel.

Index

191